HEALTH, HEALING AND TRANSFORMATION

Biblical reflections on the church
in ministries of healing & wholeness

E. Anthony Allen
Kenneth L. Luscombe
Bryant L. Myers
Eric R. Ram

MARC / WORLD VISION INTERNATIONAL

HEALTH, HEALING AND TRANSFORMATION
Biblical reflections on the Church in ministries
of healing and wholeness

E. Anthony Allen
Kenneth L. Luscombe
Bryant L. Myers
Eric R. Ram

Copyright ©1991 by MARC and World Vision International. Published by MARC and World Vision International, 919 West Huntington Drive, Monrovia, California, 91016 USA. All rights reserved. No portion of this book may be reproduced in any form, except for brief excerpts in reviews, without the written permission of the publisher.

Printed in the United States of America. First printing: May 1991. Cover Design: Edler Graphics, Monrovia, California. Cover artwork taken from a copper engraving at the Huntington Library, San Marino, California. Typography: Ventura Publisher. Body Text: Palatino 14 pts, reduced photographically to 82%.

ISBN: 0-912552-74-3

EDITOR'S NOTE

The papers in this collection were chosen from among those presented at the International Health Consultation, sponsored by World Vision International, held in Geneva, Switzerland, on November 2-9, 1989.

These particular papers were selected in order to combine four biblical reflections on *holism*, one of the major topics at the conference. In presenting the four as a unit of study it is hoped that the reader will have the opportunity to explore, as the authors have done, the inter-connectedness with which all people exist both as individuals — in body, mind and soul — and in relationship to each other. A word about the authors:

E. ANTHONY ALLEN, M.D., M. DIV., MRCPSYCH., is director of services of the Community Whole Person Health Ministry, sponsored by the Bethel Baptist Church in Kingston, Jamaica, West Indies. He is a theologian and a doctor qualified in psychiatry, who saw the need for an integrated approach to healing. In his reflection Dr. Allen brings together all facets of the human character — physical, mental, social and spiritual — in healing and wholeness.

THE REV. KENNETH L. LUSCOMBE, M. TH., is the associate director of the Office of Urban Advance at World Vision International, based in Monrovia, California, USA. Rev. Luscombe joined World Vision in 1989, coming from extensive experience in urban churches in Australia. He is an ordained Baptist minister with a forthright and ecumenical pastoral style and message.

BRYANT L. MYERS, PH. D., is vice president for Research and Development and the director of the MARC division of World Vision International, based in Monrovia, California, USA. As vice president over the Technical Services group, which includes healthcare and medical ministries, Dr. Myers has attended and occasionally facilitated at many major international conferences including the Geneva Health Consultation (1989), Lausanne II (1988) and the Oxford Conference on Christian Faith and Economics (1987).

ERIC R. RAM, PH. D., is the director of International Health at World Vision International, based in Monrovia, California, USA. Before joining World Vision, he was the director of the Christian Medical Commission in Geneva, Switzerland. He pioneered the Integrated Health Services Project in Miraj, Maharashtra, India. He is internationally known for his work and writings in health, healing and wholeness.

Table of Contents

The Church's Ministry of Healing: The Challenges to Commitment
by E. Anthony Allen

Foreword 3
Apostolic Healers Proclaiming the Total Gospel 5
Healing the Whole Person 11
On Being Empty Healers 19
Power and Authority in Healing 25
Healers in Healing Community 31
The Challenge 41

Discipleship as a Paradigm for Health, Healing and Wholeness
by Kenneth L. Luscombe

Introduction 45
Healing for a Broken World 49
Discipleship for Transformation 69
Selected Bibliography 84

Egypt to Israel: Healthcare and Sustainable Development
by Bryant L. Myers

Egypt to Israel: The Story 87
The Relationship to Healthcare 93

Compassionate Caring and Healing
by Eric R. Ram

Introduction 99
Call to Healing 101
Building a Healing Community 107

ONE

THE CHURCH'S MINISTRY OF HEALING: THE CHALLENGES TO COMMITMENT

E. Anthony Allen

FOREWORD

The church ought to be a healing community. Healing, which is supposed to be one of the church's foremost missions, is one of its most neglected.

One of the greatest reasons for this neglect is that Western-influenced churches are ignoring the biblical theological foundations of the church's healing ministry. The theological challenges to commitment in *involvement in* and *understanding of* the church's healing ministry are well summarized in Luke 9:1-4.

> *Jesus called the twelve disciples together, and gave them power and authority to drive out all demons and to cure diseases. Then he sent them out to preach the kingdom of God and to heal the sick, after saying to them, "Take nothing with you for the journey; no stick, no beggar's bag, no food, no money, not even an extra shirt. Wherever you are welcomed, stay in the same house until you leave that town."*

These challenges to the church will be shared from this text in the following series of biblical expositions:

- The challenge to be **apostolic healers proclaiming the total gospel**
- The neglect and possibilities of **healing the whole person**
- The meaning of **being empty healers**
- The possibility of **power and authority in healing**
- The need to be **healers in a healing community**

- The challenge

If we can help our local congregations, as well as the wider church, to come to grips with the theological cornerstones of healing, then we can be assured that this ministry will truly become transformed from a *neglected imperative* to an *all-out initiative*.

APOSTOLIC HEALERS PROCLAIMING THE TOTAL GOSPEL

*Then he sent them out to preach
the kingdom of God,
and to heal the sick... (Luke 9:2)*

It is unfortunate, but largely true, that the congregations of the church have abandoned healing and healthcare delivery to the medical establishment. Even where churches have been involved in medical missions, these have been relegated to medical professionals and divorced from the day-to-day mission of the local congregation.

The problem is that churches have been conditioned by the dualistic influence on Western philosophy of Descartes. He claimed that the body on the one hand and the mind and spirit on the other, though co-existing, have no influence whatsoever on each other.

Also basic to Western thought is materialism, which denies the importance or reality of the human spirit. Thus we have tended to be guilty of a "schizophrenic" or split-mind approach, isolating our members' use of medical science, as well as psychology, from the realities of spirituality and the need of the church to be a healing community.

Yet health is not the business only of the medical profession or of psychologists. It is the business also, and in fact definitively so, of the church.

If we are to take Scripture as a basis of our function, it becomes apparent from the verses in St. Luke that one theological cornerstone of commitment to the church's ministry of healing is that it is a mandate of Christ to be obeyed. This mandate comes from the very will and love of Christ. Jesus sends his disciples — and ourselves as disciples — not only to "preach the kingdom," but to "heal the sick."

What are the truths about the church's ministry of healing that face us from this text? They are: we are apostles of healing, healing is demonstrating the kingdom, and the total gospel of salvation includes healing.

We are apostles of healing

First, we are all apostles of healing. Thus we are *sent*. The Greek word for "sent" transliterated is "apostellein" which has the same root as the word "apostle." The apostles were *ones sent*; as those who are sent, we are all to be apostles of healing.

We are not our own. Once we make a commitment to Christ, it is also a commitment to those to whom he is committed. When John the Baptist questioned Jesus saying "Are you the one who should come, or should we look for another?" did he not say of himself:

> *Go and tell John what you have seen and heard; the blind receive their sight, the lame walk, lepers are cleansed, and the deaf hear; the dead are raised up, the poor have the good news preached to them. And blessed is he who takes no offense in me. (Luke 7:22-23)*

If Christ had a concern for the healing of the suffering as a central point in his *Messiahship*, how much more should we help the church to see this mission as central to our *discipleship and apostleship*?

Healing is demonstrating the kingdom of God

The second truth is that healing is demonstrating the kingdom. The disciples, and we in the church as disciples, are sent to heal as a part of our proclamation of the kingdom of God.

Preceding the challenge to heal is the charge to "preach the kingdom of God." In Luke 9:11, the healings of Christ are preceded by his proclamation. "When the crowds heard about it, they followed him. He welcomed them, spoke to them about the kingdom of God and healed those who needed it."

Too often the concept of the kingdom of God, as projected by the church in today's world, lacks relevance. This is because we do not *show* the world how the kingdom affects a person's existence in ways that can be observed or experienced.

Healing is both a sign and a manifestation of the "kingdom power" of God, working through Jesus, to bring his new order into existence. In this order "He has put all enemies under his feet" (I Cor. 15:25).

Healing is a part of the proclamation of the kingdom. The medium is the message. The ultimate goal of healing is a *sign* to point persons to the kingdom so that they may know Christ the King (or Lord) and become his subjects. Thus, healing is central to evangelism.

As a *manifestation* of the kingdom, Christ's healing shows that in the kingdom we are freed from the oppressive reign of sin, Satan and suffering, and come under the liberating, healing reign of God. Thus, if we are laborers seeking to extend God's kingdom — if we are to be truly vehicles of the kingdom in deeds as well as words — then healing is to be a part of our ministry.

How much have health and healing been a part of our proclamation and working out of God's kingdom in today's world?

The total gospel of salvation includes healing

The third truth is that in our promoting of the challenge of church members as healers who are sent, we need to remind ourselves and them that salvation is healing too.

Traditionally, we have portrayed salvation, or the kingdom, as heavily related to moral forgiveness and transformation, but hardly related to suffering. Too often we forget that the purpose of the cross was also to destroy sickness and suffering.

Here we have two concerns: first, the human being's problem of alienation and disintegration, and second, God's action of reconciliation and healing.

The person was created perfect and in God's image (Gen. 1:27). Yet, in Gen. 3, we see that the person's basic problem of sin or alienation from God leaves him or her unprotected and thus vulnerable to disease and, ultimately, death. We become vulnerable to a disintegration of self which leads to disease of the body, mind and spirit, and a disintegration of our relationships and our social justice.

The person's alienation from God leads to the problem of condemnation and spiritual guilt. Moral temptation, sins and daily guilt disrupt one's harmony of body, mind and spirit as well as harmony with others. Furthermore, the Devil's direct activity is a disintegrating force.

How does God meet the problem of the human being? Alienation and its consequences of disintegration are met by Christ's double work on the cross — forgiveness, reconciliation and redemption on the one hand and healing (re-integration) on Calvary on the other.

In Isaiah 53:4-5 the prophet tells us "...with his stripes we are healed." Guilt is met by forgiveness as well as healing of its consequences in the case of the paralytic in Mark 2:5-12. The Psalmist speaks of God's work of forgiveness and healing when he says "Bless the Lord, O my soul, and do not forget how kind he is. He forgives all my sins and heals all my diseases" (Psa. 103:2-3).

What does all of this tell us?

It confirms that *healing is inseparable from salvation* under the reign of God. Where God reigns, there is healing. Christ, therefore, gives the church an order to manifest that healing as we proclaim the Good News of the kingdom or reign of God being available for "whosoever will."

The reign of God among us and the related salvation of Christ involve our ministry of healing because the primary concern of the kingdom is the person's greatest good. Christ, in speaking of his role as the Good Shepherd of the sheep said, "I am come that they might have life, and that they might have it more abundantly" (John 10:10). This is what salvation is all about.

What is the use of preaching by itself when there are so many in our congregations and surrounding communities whose sufferings, hurts and sicknesses are being neglected?

While such preaching is going on, do leaders and members of the churches truly know who the sick and silent sufferers are in their midst and in the wider community? Are such persons being put in touch with the *total* work of God, of whom the Psalmist says, "Bless the Lord O my soul, who forgiveth thine iniquities and healeth thy diseases" (Psa. 103:3)?

We have a need to meet. This is why God, out of his love and concern, gives us a mandate and calls us to be *ones sent* to proclaim the gospel as the *total gospel*. Is this the message that we are getting across to the church? How well are we doing so?

Summary

We have seen healing relegated by the church to the medical establishment. This is because of the split-mindedness of Western thought which holds immortal the "either-or" approach to body and mind, matter and spirit — thus rejecting the "both-and" approach of biblical theology.

Just as selective primary healthcare is an obstacle to community-based health, so is our "selective theology" a barrier to the church fulfilling its ministry of healing. As disciples, *ones called*, we are also apostles of healing, *ones sent*. We are sent both to proclaim the kingdom, God's reign for our greatest good, and to demonstrate the manifestation of that kingdom by bringing about wholeness.

Healing as salvation must be expressed in word *and* deed as we proclaim a total gospel. No longer can we let the ministry of healing be a neglected imperative. Rather, we must challenge the Body of Christ and the Light of the World to make the ministry of healing, whether medical, psychological, social or divine, an all-out initiative.

God has given us a purpose. We are discovering his perspective. May he give us the passion to fulfill his purpose.

HEALING THE WHOLE PERSON

The church has a health problem. It could be said that the health problem of the church is its misunderstanding of health.

The whole-person approach to health and human development is the most needed and yet the most neglected aspect of both Western medicine and Christianity. This has led to a situation where the individuals in both disciplines have become artificially divided, dealing with various aspects of healing as completely separate entities.

The dualistic philosophy, promulgated by the philosopher Descartes, claims that the mind and body are completely independent entities, in no way affecting one another. The Western philosophy of scientific materialism seeks to negate the reality of a human spirit existing in relationship with a divine spirit. Given this situation, we need to recognize that the holistic, or *whole-person*, approach to the individual is very much rooted in the scriptures.

First, in Luke 9:1, we see where Jesus gave the disciples "power and authority to drive out all demons" on the one hand, and "to cure diseases" on the other. Besides the themes of power and authority, the other point being suggested here is that Christ recognized that in the ministry of healing there are spiritual *and* physical causes of suffering — supernatural *and* natural — pointing toward the reality of the person as a whole being.

As we reflect on the neglect and possibilities of healing of the whole person, two aspects bear consideration: first, the biblical view of the person, and second, the "wholeness" perspective of Christ's healing.

The biblical view of the person

The "spirit-body" dualism of today's Western-influenced church is alien to the biblical view of the person. When God created the person, he breathed "into his nostrils" and the person became a living *nepesh* (Gen. 2:7). This Hebrew word for "soul" speaks of the human individual as a totality rather than as a body with a soul.

In I Thessalonians 5:23, Paul prays that "the very God of peace sanctify you wholly." In so doing, he prays that "your whole spirit, soul and body be preserved blameless unto the coming of our Lord Jesus Christ." There is no place in the Bible for a "spirit-body" or "soul-body" dualism.

The existence of the mind as part of the totality of the person is also recognized by the Scriptures in Romans 12:1-2. It follows logically that if God's concern is for wholeness, so must the church be concerned about wholeness and the healing or restoration that brings about that wholeness.

In other words, the church has to span the territories of the physical, the psychological, the social and the spiritual in its concern for human beings. To do this is to call attention to the need for a ministry of healing of the whole person.

How much are our churches witnessing in their preaching, Bible teaching, evangelism and worship to the biblical view of the person? How much are we challenging the church to this task?

The wholeness perspective of Christ's healing

The encounter between Christ and the cripple, by the pool of Bethzatha, gives us a vivid demonstration of what disease is and what wholeness is:

> *Jesus saw him lying there, and he knew that the man had been ill for such a long time; so he asked him, "Do you want to get well?" The sick man answered, "Sir, I have no one here to put me in the pool when the water is stirred up; while I am trying to get in, somebody gets there first." Jesus said to him, "Get up, pick up*

your mat and walk"... Afterwards, Jesus found him in the temple and said, "Listen, you are completely well now; so stop sinning or something worse may happen to you." (John 5:6-8,14)

The following realities suggest the wholeness perspective of Christ's healing: psychological hopelessness is met by new possibilities, social alienation and oppression meet caring, and spiritual rebellion meets forgiveness and reconciliation.

Psychological hopelessness is met by new possibilities

When Christ asks the crippled man, "Do you want to get well?" or "Wilt thou be made whole?" his question reflects the first aspect of the man's disease apart from the physical — the psychological dimension. In this case, the psychological dimension involved the *hopelessness of helplessness*.

Hope is the psychological ingredient to health or wholeness. It is hope that is the mobilizer of the healing forces of the body, mind and spirit. Without a vision, the people perish — without hope, there is no purpose or meaning to living. Despair is one of the greatest causes of disease and death. Thus Christ's question "Do you want to get well?" implies that healing involves psychological motivation: *hope*.

One of the factors about disease that leads to a lack or lessening of hope is the disability that disease brings. The crippled man was giving up hope because his disability limited his receiving help.

Another factor limiting hope is that the conventional options for aiding recovery are limited. The angel came only once per year to "trouble" the water and, even then, only the first to step in would be healed. How could this cripple be the first?

Even in modern society, healthcare is limited in its availability, especially to the most ill and most socially deprived — those who are least able to find the means to afford adequate care. Conventional healthcare is limited not only in availability, but also in its potency to bring about total health.

Therefore, wisely enough, the stated goal of medicine is not mainly to cure but to *relieve suffering*. Thus, not only does the suffering and limitation of disability produce hopelessness, but also the limitation of conventional healthcare in terms of availability and potency.

Wilt thou be made whole? Or are you giving up? How aware are you of your hopelessness? How much is it contributing to your disease? These are the questions being addressed by Christ to each suffering individual, and they are the questions that the church should be addressing to all such persons.

Where there is psychological helplessness, Christ brings hope by bringing new possibilities of his divine provision. "Get up, pick up your mat, and walk," says Jesus as the answer to the hopelessness of helplessness. All things are possible to him that believes. Don't look down, look forward, have hope!

Are we in the local churches similarly challenging those in our congregations and communities in need of healing of body, mind and relationships to do this?

Social alienation and oppression meet caring

The answer that the crippled man gave to Christ's question started with the words, "Sir, I have no one here to put me in the pool...I have no one...." A caring relationship is the *social* ingredient of health or wholeness. It is the caring of another that brings about the availability of healing resources, whether medicine, counseling or miracles.

Having someone to care for us also strengthens the potency of healing resources by giving rise to a sense of belonging. The person is a social being as much as he or she is a psychological and physical being. The individual has a basic need for fellowship, listening, understanding and the affirmation of others.

In my medical and psychiatric experience, social alienation or loneliness on the one hand, and social oppression on the other, are extremely common aspects of most psychological illnesses and problems. They also contribute to several physical disorders as well. Let us remember that loneliness depends on the quality of friendship as well as the quantity of friends. One can be lonely in a crowd. To say, like the crippled man, "I have no one," is to say I have no hope for my helplessness.

But, thanks to God, there is an answer to our loneliness and social rejection. Christ was beside that man in his moment of need. Like the cripple we may feel we have no one, but Christ is also standing beside us in our moment of need. We do not have to feel the hopelessness of the helplessness of loneliness and social oppression. We can have a relationship with the caring Christ.

Don't look down; reach out! Reach out to the caring Jesus. The caring Jesus is a curing Jesus. Is this not the message of wholeness that the church should be bringing to those who are lonely and socially alienated and oppressed?

Jesus has not only a desire to care, but he has *power* in his caring. He had the authority of his supernatural power whereby he could say, "Get up, pick up your mat and walk" — and so the scriptures could say, "...and immediately the man was made whole." How, specifically, does Christ's caring relationship relate to the social aspect of disease?

The very presence of Christ meets us in the context of our social alienation, or loneliness, and our oppression. His spirit is a comfort and a compensation. He can make up for our having no one by bringing about the availability of miraculous healing resources and belonging.

Yet Christ does not always intend just for himself to compensate for loneliness and social oppression in sickness. He also provides the fellowship of the church to be the community of caring and healing through counseling, medical services and practical social action.

In this context, Christ has sent his spirit to give us the miraculous fruit of love so that we Christians can have a supernatural God-given desire to care in practical ways. He has also sent his spirit to give us his miraculous gifts of healing and faith so that we have a supernatural *power to care* through a ministry of divine healing.

"Wilt thou be made whole?" "Sir, I have no one." "Rise, take up thy bed and walk." Are you feeling loneliness in your suffering? Don't look down in hopelessness. Reach out to the caring Christ and the caring Christians. This is the challenge to each of us and also the challenge that the local churches and their members should be giving to their communities.

Let us, as Christians, be Christ's representatives through the Spirit, so that others may reach out to us in their loneliness and find the caring and curing spirit of Christ in us.

How many of us who are sick or having problems are reaching out to Jesus and to others in our search for wholeness? To what degree is the church making this a reality in its life and mission?

Spiritual rebellion meets forgiveness and reconciliation

In bringing wholeness or health to the crippled man, Christ did not just deal with the psychological aspect of hopelessness by bringing the hope of new possibilities, or with the social aspects of loneliness and oppression by developing a caring relationship. He also dealt with the third aspect of health — the spiritual dimension: "Listen, you are completely well now; so stop sinning or something worse may happen to you" (John 5:14).

Sickness has its root in sin in a general way — universally — and in specific ways within many individuals. All persons have sinned, and all have turned their backs on God. This leads to a lack of God's protection and thus a vulnerability to disease. As long as we are in sin, or as long as we sin, we will not enjoy full protection. We are vulnerable to *psychological conflicts, interpersonal conflicts, natural physical disorders and demonic or spiritual evil.*

True wholeness involves reconciliation to God, thus inviting repentance and the seeking of forgiveness on the part of the rebellious individual — "...stop sinning or something worse may happen to you."

We are never going to be truly whole until the problem of sin or our relationship with God is dealt with. We may get relief from a particular ailment or conflict, but there will never be a lasting wholeness until we receive the restoration of reconciliation to God through repentance.

When we turn our backs on our rebellion against God — and on the consequent abuse of our bodies, minds, spirits and neighbors — then we can receive forgiveness, redemption and reconciliation with God, made possible by Christ's atoning death on the cross.

When we are sick or have problems, not only must we avoid looking down in the hopelessness of helplessness, not only must we reach out in our loneliness and social alienation to the caring Christ and to his people in the fellowship of believers but, most of all, we must look up to the cross for the restoring of forgiveness and reconciliation.

How many of us look up to the cross as we seek wholeness? How much is the church challenging the sick and suffering, in both body and mind, to struggle with the unique dimension of the spiritual so that they may find ultimate freedom and, thus, wholeness?

Summary

The health problem of the church is its misunderstanding of health. The errors of Western thought have sidetracked the church from a theology of healing. Wholeness is not a sufficiently central notion to the church's ministry.

As ones sent to heal, we need to rediscover the biblical view of the person, of health and of healing as these relate to wholeness. The healing of the crippled man at the pool of Bethzatha gives us a true picture of the wholeness perspective of Christ's healing of the person.

In ministering to the *physical* illness of the man, Christ addressed the *psychological* dimension as he related to hopelessness, the *social* dimension as he met alienation with his presence and caring, and the *spiritual* dimension by calling for a change of heart from rebellion against God.

Let us therefore challenge the church and ourselves to seek to avoid the travesty of the patchwork approach to health, healing and wholeness. Let healing of the whole person — body, mind, social relationships and spirit — be not a neglected possibility, but an accessible reality.

On Being Empty Healers

One of the problems distracting the church from its ministry of healing is its inflated concern that church buildings not be empty. Rather, the church should concern itself with church leaders and members being empty of possessions and human power.

An intrinsic aspect of the kingdom or reign of God in human affairs is justice. It is to be noted that Christ did not tell his disciples to be selective about who should receive healing. Instead, his challenge to them is to avoid the temptation of making a priority of laboring for reward. Hence, the challenge to "...take nothing with you for the journey; no stick, no beggar's bag, no food, no money, not even an extra shirt..." (Luke 9:3). He is saying, "...to take nothing, to be an empty healer, gives us a freedom to serve all in justice."

As we reflect on being empty healers, three aspects come to mind: the politics of healthcare, the challenge of emptiness, and the security of emptiness.

The politics of healthcare

What about the politics of healthcare? The challenge of Christ is a far cry from the trends in modern medicine. Today, healthcare is a *commodity* rather than a *right*.

In a historical study of the medical profession in the United States, Paul Starr, historian and sociologist, claims that the rise of this "sovereign profession" and the making of this "vast industry" is due to one force — the profession's pursuit of wealth and power. In my own view, the scientific and humanitarian values of the profession have traditionally been its greatest strength, although Professor Starr's criticism is becoming increasingly true of medicine practiced everywhere.

In "The Child's Name Is Today," an overview of the status of health delivery in the world, Dr. David Morley, an authority in international community health, says that poverty and lack of education due to injustice are the greatest causes of disease in today's world. This is true despite the numerous and miraculous advances in medical technology.

Morley reports that whereas US$400 is spent per person on health in developed countries, only US$4 is spent on the average individual in the Third World. Indeed, this trend is reflected in the fact that most people in the world today do not have access to adequate healthcare. Nevertheless, within most countries, even the poorest, those of good means can enjoy almost first-rate medical care.

Medical care is increasingly the domain of the drug companies, private hospital corporations and medical technology manufacturers — not of the people. Are the poor then not like the man at the pool of Bethzatha? He waited for the annual troubling of the waters by the angel, but had no one to help him gain access to the healing waters.

How much are Christian professionals, and others who are informed, making the church aware of the politics of healthcare?

Injustice deprives persons of the resources for medical healing. It leads to the psychological stress of hopelessness and the spiritual rebellion characterized by loss of faith. Is there a challenge here for the church to seek to help guarantee quality care for the population?

Did not the prophet Isaiah highlight the meaning of the kingdom of God when he shared God's word to Israel, and to us, to put the priority not on "sabbaths, the calling of assemblies, feasts...and many prayers," but to "seek justice" and "relieve the oppressed" (Isa. 1:13-17)? This is the kingdom ministry to which we are called. But is this the ministry to which we are challenging the church?

The challenge to emptiness

What does injustice call for? It calls for a challenge to emptiness. Our faith and our understanding of our world can lead us to the following conclusions which must shape the modern challenge to our style of health and healing ministries:

- Healthcare is a political issue, not merely an economic one.

- Healthcare for the poor is a very low priority in the world now, both politically and socially.

- For the health professional to be committed to the poor is to risk being a victim personally, both economically and politically. How eloquent is the witness of a medical colleague in Latin America, tortured for three months in prison and then exiled because of his commitment to the poor.

- As Christians, our faith tells us that ministering to the poor is the church's and our greatest priority in our practical service. Even if we do not meet this demand consistently, no other single organization has such a mandate at the top of its service agenda.

For too long, Third World countries have been mission *fields* instead of becoming a mission *force*. While our own professionals are being lured away, we look to foreign First World doctors to run "band-aid, two-week clinics" for our poor.

The big question facing the health professional in today's world is "What does it mean to be a Christian disciple?" What are the economic consequences? One thing for sure is that to work for the poor is to become infected by poverty; to work on behalf of the oppressed is to become a victim of oppression.

How then can we approach health ministry economics seeking financial security and social status as a prerequisite to involvement? Christ did not tell only the rich young ruler to sell all his goods to serve the poor. He also told the disciples "Sell all your belongings and give your money to the poor" (Luke 12:33). Doesn't this sentiment apply to us as Christ's disciples?

Do we remember the brash young aspirant to discipleship who told Christ, "I will follow you wherever you go." Jesus told him, as he tells us today, "Foxes have holes, and birds have nests, but the Son of man has nowhere to lie down and rest" (Luke 9:57-58).

To be emptied is to be free. In a real sense, we can only be free to serve the sick, suffering and powerless when we are freed from having to strive for possession, status and power — when we are empty healers.

How free are we? Is this our stance as we live out our concerns? Is this the stance to which we are challenging the church?

The security of emptiness

How can we survive as empty healers — without sticks, beggar's bags, food, money or extra clothing? Is there any security in emptiness of possessions or status?

We see two clues in Luke 9. One, when Jesus says, "wherever you are welcomed, stay in the same house" (v.4), and the other in the story of the feeding of the five thousand. God provides through community and through his miraculous grace. There will always be someone in God's community to welcome us, and there will always be God's resources to feed us.

Perhaps we can have the faith of the poor elderly woman who, as she prayed for her next meal, was overheard by some passing juvenile delinquents. One of them put a loaf on her steps. When the woman saw it and rejoiced to God, the youth told her that he put the loaf there, seeking to ridicule her. She confronted him with the retort, "Young man, even the Devil himself God can use to provide for his people!"

As Christians, we are assured of God's provision if we abide in him and he in us (John 15:7). If we give all, he will give us all that we need. Thus, as apostles of healing or as ones sent to heal the whole person, we are not only empty healers. Beyond this we also have a promise of fulfillment — we have *security* in emptiness.

To talk about preaching the kingdom of God is also to live within the economy of the kingdom. After Christ exhorted his disciples "not to worry about the food you need to stay alive or about the clothes you need for your body," he reassures them that, "Your Father knows that you need these things. Instead, be concerned with his kingdom and he will provide you with these things" (Luke 12:22,30-31).

The just shall live by faith, and faith is that which is the strength of the empty healer. Faith is not blind superstition, a leap in the dark. It is to venture into the light of God's reality.

Yes, there is freedom and also security in emptiness of possessions and status. How free are we to fulfill Christ's challenge to be empty healers and thus to inherit his kingdom? Is this the challenge that we are giving to the church?

Summary

Because healthcare tends to be a commodity rather than a right, the politics of healthcare dictate that the poor will have the least access to it. The highest service priority of the church is to the poor. Healing involves a struggle against injustice by making the necessary resources available to the poor. The rewards system is such that those who serve the poor risk poverty themselves. Yet, to be empty healers is to have complete freedom to serve Christ. To be empty is to be secure. To be empty is to inherit the kingdom.

POWER AND AUTHORITY IN HEALING

One of the biggest obstacles to the fulfillment of the ministry of healing in the life of our congregations is the lack of appreciation of both the scale of the battle and the scope of our resources.

Ministering wholeness to the broken, hope to the depressed, reconciliation to the alienated and deliverance to the bound is an awesome task. The battle is as much spiritual as it is strictly medical, psychological or social.

Some of us plunge in uninformed and become casualties in our ignorance. Others of us have a "head" or intellectual awareness of the task, but are spiritually ill-equipped. We fall by the wayside or become too broken to heal because within our hearts our vision of God is too small.

The source of power that is peculiar to the church and its members, as the disciples of God, is that which Christ confers. It is stated in our key passage of St. Luke, when Christ gave his disciples "power and authority to drive out all demons and to cure diseases" (Luke 9:1). As we reflect on the possibility of power in healing, we can then examine the following related themes: the nature of the battle, the kingdom and possibilities of power, and the imbuement of power.

The nature of the battle

What about the precise nature of the battle?

In our healing ministry of counseling, medical services, prayer and social action, ministering to the spiritual relationship of the person to his or her maker is the most difficult aspect because it is the person's area of greatest resistance to wholeness. Evil forces in this world compete for the spiritual loyalty of the individual. Forces operate in the psyche to tempt us to the deadly sins of egoism, lust, pride, envy, avarice, hatred, deceit, injustice and the idolatry of materialism.

As a psychiatrist, I have witnessed evil in the psyche in counseling a young woman who was raped by a pastor she trusted. The pastor then encouraged an abortion, leaving the woman with a legacy of guilt, outrage and shame. I have witnessed the fear of a wife whose church elder husband brutalized her. I have also witnessed the rage of persons who mutilated the faces of their partners with acid.

Not only do we face the demons of the psyche but also demons in the world's socio-political orders — unbridled capitalism, racism, rightist fascism, and totalitarian communism. I believe demonic forces of the psyche and social orders are attacking us in the form of a new tyranny in the family, where abuse of all types is rapidly becoming commonplace.

Whether we are believers or not in the potency of occult evil, such as witchcraft, which is found in all cultures, we cannot deny the bondage of fear, fatalism and hate that it produces. In the West we see Satanist cults, and elsewhere we hear of "hex deaths" which defy explanation by scientists.

Those of us who are not blinded by the rationalism of the West and who have truly explored the darkest reaches of human existence will have no doubt about the relentless power of autonomous evil forces. A story is told that during a strategy planning session, Satan and his demons were hard put to find a foolproof plan to gain a stronger foothold on earth. Imagine Satan's delight when a seemingly insignificant demon came up with what has been the most powerful strategy ever. "Sir," the demon suggested, "let us first of all delude humans into believing that we do not exist!"

The study and use of parapsychology is a well known concomitant to technology in wars between nations, as exemplified by Adolf Hitler in World War II. Indeed, St. Paul warns the Christians at Ephesus that "We are not fighting against human beings but against the wicked spiritual forces in the heavenly world, the rulers, authorities, and cosmic powers of this dark age" (Ephesians 6:12).

Though we need to be healers who are empty of possessions and status, no one can prescribe love, virtue and hope when the power is nonexistent. Healers are wounded too. They also can become corrupt. Physicians are among the greatest victims of suicide and drug addiction. All who are in the healing professions or function in volunteer roles would have to admit to some aspect of brokenness.

What about corruption? I have seen patients who have reported being sexually abused by doctors claiming to do sex therapy. Dr. Mengele, a Nazi, was considered a skilled physician, yet he was a practitioner of genocide. Many "Mengeles" exist today in both the North and the South in the service of totalitarianism.

To what extent are we going to take up the challenge to bring about a new awareness of the true nature of the battle, in the various aspects of our ministry to the whole person in community? How much will we help to make the church aware?

The kingdom and the possibilities of power

The kingdom brings possibilities of power. To be recipients of God's power is the difference between potential and performance.

In our ministry of praying for and tending to sick individuals and families, communities, nations and a sick world, God gives us power to transcend the limitations of science in dealing with the spiritual diseases of persons that Satan inflicts.

Jesus saw his healing ministry in terms of the kingdom of God, or God's reign of liberating power. In Luke 9:11, the healings of Christ are preceded by his proclamation of the kingdom. His commandment to his disciples in Luke 9:2 is "to preach the kingdom of God and heal the sick." This was after he "gave them power and authority over all devils to cure diseases" (Luke 9:1). In the Beelzebub controversy, Christ asserts that "If I cast out devils by the Spirit of God, then the kingdom of God is come unto you" (Luke 11:20).

Healing is both a sign and a manifestation of the "kingdom power" of God, working through Jesus to bring his new order into existence. In this order "He has put all enemies under his feet" (I Cor. 15:25); the Greek word "dunamis" is used for power, having the same root as the word "dynamite." This usage is most apt, for Christ said, "With men it is impossible; but with God all things are possible" (Matthew 19:26).

The power of Christ was given not only over the supernatural, but also over natural evil — the power to cure diseases. Many natural diseases, though understood, still today have no cure. When we believe we have cornered all natural disease, some new strain of virus or disorder of the environment is inflicted upon us. Ultimately, only God has absolute power over nature and natural evil. We need his power to heal those who are sick of natural and supernatural causes.

As ones sent, how much of a place are we going to give to the recognition of divine resources in our health and healing mission? How much are we going to challenge the church to receive this power?

The imbuement of power

This *dunamis* that Christ gave to his disciples is available to all who serve the sick and oppressed. It comes through Christ's atoning death and his triumphal resurrection. It comes through the daily spiritual guidance and the exercise of his spiritual gifts that come when we daily submit to the Holy Spirit (I Cor. 13).

Most of all, power and authority come by prayer. Let us not forget the experience of futility the disciples had as they battled with the disease of the epileptic boy. They asked Jesus, "Why couldn't we drive the demon out?" Jesus answered, "It was because you haven't enough faith...I assure you that if you have faith as big as a mustard seed, you can say to this hill, 'Go from here to there!' and it will go." Some manuscripts include,

"But only prayer and fasting can drive this kind out; nothing else can" (Matt. 17:20-21, Mark 9:29).

God's power is nothing that we merit or "work toward." It is liberating to know that our effectiveness in ministry is not dependent on our inconsistent and limited power, but rather on God's power. It is part of his free gift of grace which he gives in love and which we attain only through acceptance and faith. In a sense, to have power is to become as a little child in our prayer of faith.

How much have we accepted Christ's power and authority? How much do we need to challenge the church once more to find its dynamism?

Summary

Healing, through whatever means, is as much a spiritual as a physical and interpersonal battle. Anything less than a spiritually undergirded approach to the ministry of healing by the church will result in mere patchwork efforts and defeat. It can also wound and corrupt the healers.

Christ's order to be obeyed does not have to do with the mere replication of one-sided medical or psychological and social approaches. Any honest expert in these fields will readily admit that these are but a limited aspect of the care of persons.

God provides for mankind the biblical model of wholeness. He also provides the resources which enable us to combine all of the medicine and counseling approaches. We need to practice them with the undergirding of prayer for God's divine power in healing natural diseases and for authority over spiritual bondage. Healers sent are healers equipped.

For the neglected imperative of God's healing ministry to become an all-out initiative of the church, we need not only a purpose, a wholeness perspective and a passion. We also need power.

Let us open our minds, hearts and spirits for God to give us that power of his Spirit in our prayer and faith. Let us challenge the church of today once more to claim the *power* that gave it birth.

HEALERS IN HEALING COMMUNITY

One of the greatest causes of failure in the church's health and healing ministry is the positioning of congregations as theaters instead of healing communities. Chapels with platforms as stages for the clergy and robed choirs to perform on are too often more the order of the day than are organic communities where each person is as important as the other and each has a friend.

We cannot heal in isolation. We need others. This is demonstrated in Jesus' words to his disciples that while they should take nothing for the journey, "...wherever you are welcomed, stay in the same house until you leave that town" (Luke 9:3-4).

As one reflects on the need for the church to be a healing community, there are three themes that we need to consider: the potential of the group, love and justice as motivators, and practical ways of being community.

The potential of the group

Beyond our need for others as individuals, the group has healing powers that are greater than the sum of the healing powers of its members. A dying man called his twelve feuding sons together. How could he unify them? He asked each to get two sticks. On his instruction, each son easily broke one of the sticks. Then he asked them to bind the twelve remaining sticks together and then try to break the bundle. The sons indeed got the message that the whole is greater than the sum of the parts. The strength of the church is in its unity.

Another value of the church as a group is its function of support. It is now recognized that occupational burnout is a special hazard of those engaged in human services. It is also established that formal and informal professional and personal support groups are among the best protectors against burnout.

Christ himself faced burnout in Gethsemane and at several other points of his ministry (Matt. 26:38). He also needed a healing group. So do all today who minister to others. We were all born in groups. Few significant human achievements have taken place without a group effort.

In Exodus 18:13-27, we see that Moses "was kept busy from morning till night" settling disputes among the Israelites. Jethro, his father-in-law, said to him,

> *Why are you doing this all alone?...You are not doing this the right way. You will wear yourself out and these people as well...You should choose some capable men and appoint them as leaders of the people; leaders of thousands, hundreds, fifties and tens...Let them serve as judges of people on a permanent basis. They can bring all the difficult cases to you, but they themselves can decide all the smaller disputes. That will make it easier for you.*

Jethro was perhaps the first "management consultant." With its strength in unity, its value of support and its potential for efficiency in task fulfillment through sharing of responsibilities, the church as a group has great potential for healing.

How great is the challenge we are giving to the church and our congregations to use this potential?

Love and justice as motivators

When we look beyond the needs of the world's suffering, poor and bound, we need to ask ourselves what the motivating force is behind the church being a community of healing.

Love is the greatest motivator for healing in and by the congregation. God heals simply because he loves. Love is the greatest commandment. It motivates concern for others. This concern demands action in caring where there is sickness and suffering. The apostle John exhorts the early church and ourselves today:

> *We know that we have left death and come over into life; we know it because we love our brothers...This is how we know what love is...Christ gave his life for us. We, too, then ought to give our life for the brothers... It must be true love which shows itself in action. (1 John 3:14,16,18)*

So often when I counsel patients going through broken relationships I discover that they had a mistaken notion of love. To them, saying "I love you" meant "I want to possess you and to depend on you." We will recall that as Job lost his possessions and several loved ones, scripture states that, "Then, after Job had prayed for his friends, the Lord made him prosperous again and gave him twice as much as he had before" (Job 42:10-11).

Love is unconditional and one of the greatest healing forces. In the case of the Good Samaritan, when a neighbor is encountered new challenges of unconditional love in the church's ministry of health and healing are discovered.

Justice and equal distribution of healthcare are also what summons us into healing communities. Love demands concern. The prophet Isaiah proclaims God's challenge that religious concern demands justice (Isa. 53:6-8). Injustice is a transgression of the law and thus is a sin. This sin leads to disease — the absence of physical, mental, social and spiritual well-being.

The church should seek to mobilize all members of its congregations to carry out justice in healthcare. Also, as "salt" and "light" (Matt. 5:13-16), Christians should proclaim "health justice" as part of the gospel. This action and proclamation will be in the context of given socio-political forms of oppression which need to be identified, repudiated and exposed as being against God's law. They also need to be met with Christian alternatives.

To minister to the "least" as well as to the greatest of those who are sick is to minister to Christ (Matt. 25:33-40). How much are we encouraging the church to face the challenge of being motivated by love and justice to be a healing community?

Practical ways of being community

How does the biblical theology of the church inform practical challenges with regard to the church being a healing community?

In its obedience, the local church should seek to become a community of concerned believers, acting in response to the needs of each and all. Out of encounter with the church should come wholeness because of unity and respect. Too often, the needs of each and all fail to be met because prejudice and condescension exist. They act like cancers, destroying unity and respect in the church. St. Paul said,

> *So then you gentiles are not foreigners or strangers any longer; you are now fellow citizens with God's people and members of the family of God...you too are built upon the foundation laid by the angels and the prophets, the cornerstone being Christ Jesus himself. (Eph. 2:19-20)*

Conversion and initiation into the church is an initiation into a personal and corporate life of sharing. Out of this sharing a therapeutic environment is created where we "bear one another's burdens..." (Gal. 6:2); "rejoice with them that do rejoice, and weep with those that weep" (Romans 12:15).

In Acts 4:32 we see that as members of the early church were filled with the Holy Spirit, "the group of believers was one in mind and heart. No one said that any of his belongings was his own, but they all shared with one another everything they had."

The therapeutic church community is one that prays for God to heal in its midst (Acts 4:30) and where members confess faults to one another and pray for one another's healing (James 5:16). As with the men who let down the palsied man through the roof, the faith of the congregation will receive Christ's attention.

One aspect of a person's physical and psychological wholeness is his social integration into a human fellowship. Yet another aspect is one's integration with God, who is the major integrating force. Total integration cannot occur without these two realities.

Thus, the church community has a responsibility to promote each person's psychological and physical integration and economic welfare by ensuring that his or her needs in the areas of fellowship and spirituality are met. The church community as a therapeutic community is a "total care" community, as in the command to "do good to all men, especially unto them who are of the household of faith" (Gal. 6:10).

The local church as a hospital

There are certain elements of the local congregation which are therapeutic and are not found in a secular environment. These include: (1) a fellowship formed by the Holy Spirit (Eph. 2:18-22), (2) gifts of the Spirit for ministry, (3) proclamation of the gospel as Good News of grace, (4) teaching for Christian growth, and most important, (5) prayer, the ritual of access to God. In all these activities, the church is directed and empowered by the Holy Spirit (John 14:26, Acts 1:8). With all these elements, the congregation has something unique to offer to the world in its ministry of healing.

Instead of the church being represented by the image of a theater or stage, it should be envisioned as a hospital — a place not merely for the drama of preaching and ritual, but primarily for the healing of the sick.

Once, while talking to a minister friend of mine about a member of his congregation whom I was seeing professionally, we reflected on how his church, practically, could be supportive of this psychologically ill patient. I recall him saying, "You know, doctor, so often it seems that in the church we seem to pay more attention to those who are well than to those who are sick."

In its stewardship, the local congregation as a healing community should mobilize all of its talents and resources. God is a God of medicines, persons and miracles. He has given us the materials and skills in the church to carry out a medical ministry. Christ himself pointed to the need for medicines when he said that it is those who are sick who have need for a physician (Mark 2:17).

The model of the church member as village health worker and community organizer is an apt and necessary one. The main goal that the World Health Organization has set for this planet is "Health for All by the Year 2000."

What healthcare experts are saying is that this justice in healthcare can only come about in the context of integrated communities where each person takes responsibility for the health of the other. If all local congregations worldwide in every city, town and village took this mandate seriously and trained at least two members to work as lay community health workers, then there would be a health revolution on our planet.

Christ has given us human resources to exercise skills in counseling services. In Galatians 6:2, Paul exhorts us to bear one another's burdens in this area. There are many in our local communities and congregations who are suffering from anxiety, depression or personality problems; from difficulties with marriages, children, jobs, finances, sexuality or relationships in general.

Daily we face the crises of death, divorce, and loneliness, and daily we need to respond. Beyond this, if it is consistent to its mandate, only the church may be able to generate the total social commitment needed to rehabilitate those most neglected by society such as the addicted, the mentally ill and the homeless of all our countries.

Spiritual aspects also need to be addressed by counseling. These might include the need to make a commitment to Christ and to experience his Spirit, or possibly a loss of faith, doubt or hopelessness, discernment of God's will or experiencing a feeling of distance from God.

The counseling ministry is one that health professionals, as well as non-professionals — ministers and lay leaders included — can perform. All church members can engage in informal counseling. This can be done in home visitations or on the occasions of life changes, ordinances and religious ceremonies, such as funerals, weddings, the blessing of children or baptisms.

Prayer as a tool for healing

Beyond all of this, Christ has given to his church the most powerful tool for holistic healing. This is prayer. The apostle James makes it abundantly clear that it is the inescapable duty of elders and also of each member to pray for the sick in the congregation. He says "Is there any sick among you? Let him call for the elders of the church; and let them pray over him... Confess your faults, one to another, and pray for one another that ye may be healed" (James 5:13-16).

We in the church cannot call ourselves followers of Christ and yet be skeptical about God's ability to heal miraculously as a result of our prayers, alongside his ability to transform the person as a result of our evangelism. Each church should have groups that intercede for the sick, teams that go out to pray for the sick at home and in hospitals. There should be prayers for the sick in the liturgy of worship. The opportunities for this ministry are many.

To what degree are we engaging in a ministry of healing to the whole person in our congregations and health missions? How much are we promoting this in national and international health programs?

It is at this point of stewardship that the church cannot afford to differentiate between its natural and supernatural resources. Too often, churches take the side of providing either "secular-style" medical services on one hand or prayers and charismatic healing (use of spiritual gifts) on the other, with little effort to use both as God-given resources in healing.

Both medicine and divine healing, as well as counseling, are God's avenues to the healing of body, mind, spirit and social problems. All of these resources from God are to be equally honored and used in our stewardship of healing.

A *total ministry* of "medicines, persons and miracles" needs to involve fellowship-building activities in small groups, house groups, support groups and enrichment groups for singles, married couples, the elderly, etc. This total ministry of the church as a healing community is not only for its members, but also can be part of a community-based approach.

Let us also remember that those who heal should not be marginalized by the church. Nor should they distance themselves out of frustration with the church's failures. They, too, need the total healing community.

Summary

To neglect community is to neglect the life-blood of the church's healing ministry. Christ is the author, but community is the context. Unfortunately, too many in the ministry of healing are in the church "in spite of it" and not because they find a truly supportive community. With regard to many of our congregations, Shakespeare could have said "all the *church* is a stage."

Biblical concepts relating to the person portray the individual as a whole. The concept relating to God's saving action goes beyond forgiveness and redemption to include healing. This is the work of the cross and of the Holy Spirit, acting in the church community. God's kingdom is one in which there is wholeness.

The church as a group has strength in unity, a supportive function and efficiency in sharing. The healing ministry, however, is not to be over-emphasized to the expense of knowing Christ as Lord. Rather, the former leads to the latter. In its evangelism the church seeks healing out of love and a sense of justice and obedience to God.

The Body of Christ works as a spirit-directed therapeutic community with a total ministry, responding to the needs of all without prejudice and entering into a corporate life of sharing. It is to use all of its resources — medical skills, counseling, prayer and gifts for healing and fellowship — in its ministry of healing and restoring wholeness.

Will the modern church once more discover her essential role?

THE CHALLENGE

The challenge to the church is to be a healing community. We have seen that healing, which is supposed to be one of the church's foremost missions, is in actual practice one of its most neglected. It is evident that a significant reason for this neglect is the ignoring, by Western-influenced churches, of the biblical and theological foundations of the church's healing ministry.

The theological challenges to commitment in *involvement in* and *understanding of* the church's healing ministry, as summarized in Luke 9:1-4, have been discussed. But what can we do individually and collectively?

> The challenge goes out to members of the church to be apostolic healers proclaiming the total gospel.
>
> *Let us go, regardless!*
>
> The existing need and possibility of healing the whole person is very real.
>
> *Let us practice the whole-person approach to healing, regardless!*
>
> We have examined the need for being empty healers in our health missions.
>
> *Let us sacrifice, regardless!*

The possibility of power and authority in healing exists for each Christian and congregation.

Let us pray for power, regardless!

We are confronted by the need for God's people to be healers in a healing community.

Let us work to be and to build community, regardless!

If we can help our local congregations, as well as the wider church, come to grips with the theological cornerstones of healing, then we can be assured that this ministry will truly become transformed from a *neglected imperative* to an *all-out initiative*.

This is our task at this time. Let us seek to be more attentive and obedient to God's Word, so that we can more effectively share the message of health, healing and wholeness as intrinsic to the Good News of God's salvation to men and to women.

Two

DISCIPLESHIP AS A PARADIGM FOR HEALTH, HEALING AND WHOLENESS

Kenneth L. Luscombe

INTRODUCTION

If there is one subject that occupies a central place in the thoughts of men and women today it is the subject of health, healing and wholeness. In a world marked by deep divisions of class, color and creed, a common cause is found — the search for an existence more deserving of the term "human."

For the majority of the earth's inhabitants the problem is circumscribed by a daily struggle for survival. Disease and death are ever-present realities for millions of families. Women and children are particularly vulnerable. Women give their strength tilling the soil, preparing meals, caring for the family, and harvesting the fertility of their own bodies.

Children who survive their infancy give their strength to the informal armies that provide food for the family and protection for the community. We are all familiar with the disturbing scenes of children scavenging in the garbage heaps of the world's cities or bearing arms in the struggle for liberation.

Not so for the privileged of the earth. Life is abundant. Choice is a way of life. But accumulation can become a burden, and choice can become overwhelming. A loss of simplicity is also a loss of innocence. We are bound to choose, and in choosing we reveal our inner selves.

Vulnerability, anxiety and restlessness accompany the abundant life. Ease becomes "dis-ease." Not hungry, we overeat. Not satisfied with what we have, we overspend. Not fulfilled, we overwork. To compensate for our sins of indulgence we fret, fast, and work out at fitness centers. Health becomes another commodity in the marketplace, a means for securing prestige, pleasure and power. Dare we question whether this obsession with health is wholesome and healing?

With some urgency, then, we ask, *what does it mean to be healthy?* What are the indicators of wholeness? How can the brokenness of our world be healed? May we talk of health, healing and wholeness with any meaning while we, as members of the human community, allow 15 million of our children under the age of five to die each year because of a lack of food, clean water, basic medicines and safe housing?

The commitment of the World Vision Partnership is expressed in the statement of "core values." The first of these core values is the affirmation *"we are Christian."* We are part of the people of God whose task is to make concrete and visible in the world God's passionate concern for the ultimate healing and restoration of all creation. The principal metaphor for understanding the activity of God in the world is the "kingdom of God."

The vision of the kingdom of God is of a creation brought to wholeness and a society in which the values of justice, peace and joy in relationships prevail. No one is excluded. This kingdom receives its clearest explication in Jesus of Nazareth — in his life, death and resurrection. To be "Christian" is to invest our lives in the same things in which Jesus invested his. This is the call to discipleship that is fundamental to the Christian life.

The final core value is *"we are responsive."* This involves a commitment and a readiness to act when the situation demands, particularly in the face of life-threatening emergencies. It also means a willingness to engage in serious and critical reflection on the context of our action.

To be responsive is to be committed to the world in which we live and to the contemporary struggle for an authentic humanity. This involves the exacting task of creating and experimenting with paradigms, or models of understanding, which illuminate the Christian vision for our world and for our times. It also involves a willingness to enter into conversation with others in a community of inquiry that seeks to advance our understanding of health, healing and wholeness.

This leads me to my contention that *discipleship is a paradigm for health, healing and wholeness.* I will deal with this subject in two parts. First, I will contend that we live in a broken world desperately in need of healing, and that the Christian faith, as essentially a relational vision, has the resources to meet this need. Second, I will look at the gospel imperative to follow Jesus in discipleship as a way to transform life individually and communally in accordance with the values of the kingdom of God.

HEALING FOR A BROKEN WORLD

We live in a time when overwhelming changes are taking place throughout the world. Traditional cultures are undergoing significant transformation as they come into ever closer proximity with other cultures.

No one today is immune to the influences of change. In this volatile climate, worldviews that have been the mainstay of traditional cultures are breaking down. Pluralism and radical questioning of all claims to unqualified authority by individuals or institutions are signs of the times.

This is particularly true in the West. Over the past several centuries, commonly called the "modern era," Western culture has been undergoing a process of change driven by a commitment to scientific discovery and technological development. The impetus came from the renewal of the human spirit and creativity during the Renaissance and the Protestant Reformation, in a period of transition from the Dark Ages to the Age of Enlightenment.

The Renaissance was a cultural revival in the West prompted by the intellectual stirrings of the late Middle Ages, notably in the work of the Humanists. A secular lay movement, Renaissance Humanism retrieved and celebrated the achievements of human culture and championed the nobility and potential of the human spirit when freed from the tutelage of religious authority. The Humanists promoted a Neo-Platonic worldview discriminating between the realms of "matter" and "spirit." *What matters is the natural world, as opposed to the real, but relatively unimportant, supernatural world.*

Reformation thinking achieved a radical break with the superstitious and fate-ridden religious worldview of popular medieval Christianity. Emphasizing God's providential care in human history and his personal interest in the daily concerns of individuals, the Reformers restored appreciation for the dignity, worth and meaning of human existence and endeavor.

In their concern to develop a strong theology of providence, however, they accentuated the distinction between God and the world. *God is the divine Creator, Sustainer and Ruler of the universe. The created realm is dependent upon God for its very existence. God remains beyond the world for the sake of the world.*

The Enlightenment intensified the demand for critical, autonomous, rational thinking. Max Weber later called it the "disenchantment of the world." Given the influence of dualistic thinking on the emerging worldview, it was but a short step to effect the isolation of God in the "above." In the "below," people were learning to live without God as scientists explained more and more of the natural world without recourse to the supernatural.

The dualistic worldview and human progress

Human intelligence, not divine inspiration, shaped the secular worldview. Human ingenuity, not divine intervention, accounted for human progress. Many modern intellectuals believed that the rigorous application of scientific methods to human and natural reality would surely bring about progress toward the enlightened individual and, thereby, the good society. The age of progress, prosperity and peace was at hand.

Modern urban industrial society is the outworking of these forces for change. That significant advances have been made in the promotion of human well-being is beyond dispute. The achievements of science and technology, particularly in the medical field, have been breathtaking. Nonetheless, recent history has largely dispelled the optimism upon which the modern period was based.

Critical, rational thinking alone has not achieved widespread personal enlightenment and social liberation. The world is better understood, but it is not thereby a better world. Indeed, science and technology, pressed into service to meet the needs of Western society with its blind commitment to individualism, have deepened, rather than alleviated, human brokenness. The urban industrial milieu is tragically flawed.

The Enlightenment model of the autonomous thinker, freed from the oppressive tutelage of religious traditions, mythologies and nostrums, ironically fell prey to the charge of "illusion." A whole new battery of myths were created to replace the old: unending progress, unlimited growth, a bright new world.

Before too long the "myth of progress" began to pale. Along with a plethora of goods, scientists also fashioned tools of global destruction, thereby adding grim potential to the yet unresolved tensions in the human community. Technological progress was gained at the expense of other human values.

Similarly, commitment to the "myth of the individual" proved untenable. Scientists do not work in a neutral and value-free zone, nor are they free of the pervasive influences that history, culture and tradition exert on the individual. The self-referencing of the Enlightenment model proved to be both inadequate and dangerous. Science is not an end in itself, but part of a larger community faced with the challenge of building a just, equitable and sustainable society.

For our purposes, however, the most dangerous legacy of modern Western culture is the dualistic worldview that threatens to tear our world apart. Reality is divided and hierarchically arranged into dominant and subservient entities — rich and poor, male and female, white and black, and so forth.

At every turn we are asked to choose between body and soul, individual and community, order and freedom, power and love, God and the world, work and leisure, subject and object, fact and value, science and religion and so forth, as if these were irreconcilable opposites. In choosing, we perpetuate a way of life that fosters domination, manipulation, alienation and competition. At the heart of the question of health, healing and wholeness lies the dilemma of a fragmented world caught in a crisis of meaning and values.

If the modern era is characterized by differentiation, then the emerging post-modern world is characterized by what Martin E. Marty calls a "wholeness hunger." The agenda has shifted from self-realization to self-transcendence, from the rugged individual to the individual-in-community.

What we need is a global vision adequate to the sensibilities of our post-modern times, one that is holistic and inclusive of all reality and one that gives due recognition to the radical interdependence of all life — a relational vision. What are some of the parameters of experience within which a relational vision can be developed?

This would seem an appropriate point at which to turn to the Christian tradition in order to spell out a vision of wholeness and healing for a broken world. Healing is an integral part of the church's ministry. Nevertheless, the Western church is deeply implicated in the very institutions, systems and life styles that are in question today. Theology also participates in the global crisis to the extent that it provides support for these systems and structures.

In popular Christianity, much of the present-day revival in faith healing is linked with excessive individualism and a "theology of success" that glorifies abundance, holds suffering as evidence of poor faith, and looks askance at Christians committed to a life style of simplicity, self-denial and solidarity with the poor.

There is much in the church that is in need of unmasking and healing. Recognition and acceptance of the essential woundedness of the church is an appropriate starting point for looking at the contribution of the Christian faith to the question of health, healing and wholeness.

Salvation and becoming fully human

As was stated at the outset, the primary concern is to find an existence more truly deserving of the term "human." There can be no doubt that the ultimate goal of the religious life, as portrayed in the Bible, is to become what God created us to be:

that is, fully human. To be fully human is to experience the salvation of God. What does this mean?

The idea of *salvation* carries several nuances. There is the notion of "being saved" in the sense of being rescued, or being saved *from* some peril or threat. The Greek word in the New Testament for "save" certainly carries this meaning. But it also carries the meaning "to prosper" or "to thrive." Here the emphasis is not so much on being saved from something as it is on *what* is saved. The *what* is important to our discussion.

Western theology has been profoundly influenced by Greek speculative philosophy with its dualistic distinction between the eternal, spiritual and unchanging truth and the temporal, material and changing world. The essence, or the *what*, of the true human being and, therefore, the goal of being truly human belongs to the spiritual and eternal (soul, spirit, mind).

This entity, as an immortal substance, exists apart from the condition of material and temporal existence (body, flesh, community). The perfection of the human being is the salvation of this immortal "soul." In traditional theological terms, the task or ministry of the church is to save the soul from hell for heaven, one by one.

The unfortunate consequence of this understanding of what it means to be human is that it leads to a permanent splitting of the human being. It devalues bodily existence in the here and now, ignores the social dimension of human experience and promotes an inward and private view of spirituality. In other words, it does not move us any further in our search for a relational vision.

The Bible, however, provides us with an alternative starting point. The Old Testament is no less than the story of a community struggling to understand its calling as a people chosen by God to be a means of healing for all the nations. Here is an inclusive vision played out as a *salvation history* — the history of a particular people in a particular place in creative tension with God. What does this story have to tell us about being human?

God creates. And within creation, God creates again — male and female in God's own image. Humanity bears the divine imprint, not just as a disembodied soul, a spark of divinity locked up in the flesh, but as a living, breathing, moving being — a person. God speaks. The creature responds. Humanity is aware of the presence of God, aware of being personally addressed and aware that to flee his presence is ultimately an impossibility (Psalm 139).

The Creator cannot be understood apart from creation. Humanity, as the crown of God's good creation, is fulfilled by being in relationship with God. Creation spills over into a dynamic, relational process of creativity and co-creation.

In the Old Testament, therefore, creatureliness is an integral part of being human. It is the recognition that what we have and what we are is given by God's grace and is beyond our manipulation. Creatureliness is to be aware of the contingency of life. The created cannot replace the Creator. That is idolatry.

Furthermore, creatureliness implies that the individual person is bound to the whole of creation in a "dialogical existence." It is not good that man should be alone. Man is complemented and completed by woman. A dialogue partner is created and a song of jubilation breaks out (Genesis 2:23). Man, as male and female, is then made responsible for naming the other living creatures. Language is created. To be human is to be a constitutive part of the whole creation and to be in relationship — with God, with nature and with one another.

To be *human* is to be in the world as a responsible partner in the creative process. The individual is a person who is in the process of *becoming*. To become *more fully human* includes the risk and responsibility of freedom. To a very real extent, the individual is what he or she freely chooses to be. But freedom is never absolute. We are unavoidably conditioned by our environment, culture, family, friends and education, and by the choices we have already made.

Freedom, faith and the community

Freedom is presupposed whenever we speak of a person's responsibility in the process of becoming. Freedom is actualized as one dares to choose for the future. Freedom "takes a gamble" on life. In choosing, one runs the risk of winning or losing life. This step into the future says that life is more than sheer necessity or blind fate. It also says that hope and faith are necessary dimensions to being human. But what does that imply?

First, it implies that we are called upon to live freely and responsibly in the world. To live responsibly means to commit ourselves to a course of life that is based upon, and transparent of, the values we find to be most meaningful, worthwhile and satisfying. We are free to choose, but we are not free not to choose.

Peter Berger has called this the "heretical imperative" — imperative in that we must choose, and heretical in that in choosing we discriminate between possible choices. Since we are limited beings, we cannot choose to do and be everything. To choose one path is to close ourselves off to other paths.

Second, we can only travel one road at a time. But which road should we choose? Obviously we cannot personally experience all that is to be experienced in life and then, on the basis of our personal experience, choose the most satisfying option. We are thrown beyond ourselves to receive intimations from the experience of others. We rely on what Juan Luis Segundo calls "transcendent data," or data from beyond the self.

Third, we place our faith in the experience of men and women whose judgments we trust. These people become an example to us of a meaningful way to live. We trust their testimony. We embrace their values. We emulate their commitments. Their witness becomes a reference point for us at certain stages along the road we have chosen to travel. The examples may change, but the need to place our faith in the faith of others remains.

Fourth, given the limits of personal experience and our need for exemplars, we are bound to recognize the social nature of all experience. The individual belongs to a social network of human relationships. We are dependent upon others as we journey through life. We are thrown into existence as the culmination of many prior choices and decisions. Our personal story is inextricably bound up with the larger story of our culture, our family, our friends, our country. Likewise, our decisions also have consequences for others. The individual is radically social.

Fifth, faith is an inescapable component of what it means to be human. Without faith it is impossible to structure our life in any meaningful way. Faith is the vehicle of self-transcendence, enabling us to enter into a wider community of meaning, values and the ability to learn and grow. Faith is dynamic. It develops as life becomes more complex and our choices become more difficult.

By faith we integrate the experiences of others who have learned to solve life's problems in a satisfying way. To this extent faith is also painful. Faith that is sufficient for one stage in our personal development will not necessarily suffice at a later stage. The journey of faith, as the journey toward maturity, will involve consolidation, vulnerability, disintegration and renewed risk. Growth involves change, and change is always painful.

Sixth, faith development requires community. It is in community that we learn to trust and be trusted. Community becomes a holding environment in which the painful passage of growth can occur. Vulnerability is possible within the supportive matrix of a community. It is in community that we learn how to learn. It is in community that our identity is given and grows. It is in community that values are transferred and tested. It is in community that we are made accountable for our actions and encouraged in our efforts. Community is indispensable to meaningful existence.

Lastly, social experience has an intrinsically religious dimension. Community is the matrix wherein a person transcends the idolatry of self-serving individualism and is positioned for an encounter with transcendence. Faith confesses

Salvation is healing

If the diabolic tearing apart of reality is known as "sin," then the symbolic healing and restoration of reality is what we call "salvation." Theologian Paul Tillich has said that salvation can be described as the act of "cosmic healing:"

> The Greek word *soteria* is derived from *saos;* the Latin word *salvatio* from *salvus;* the German word *Heiland* from *heil,* which is akin to the English word *healing. Saos, salvus,* and *heil* mean whole, not yet split, not disrupted, not disintegrated, and therefore healthy and sane ... Salvation is basically and essentially healing, the reestablishment of a whole that was broken, disrupted, disintegrated.

Tillich's perspective enables us to place the question of health, healing and wholeness in the context of ultimate meaning — of the transcendent answer to the universal problem of evil.

The concept of *salvation* is clearly central to our quest for health, healing and wholeness. So far we have said that the brokenness of life is radical and inclusive. The Bible speaks of this brokenness as the result of sin. Sin is the broken relationship between the creator and the creature as a result of human rebellion. It includes both the fact of sin and the acts of sin.

Salvation, in the context of sin, is the restoration to wholeness of that which is fragmented, the healing of that which is damaged, and the health of that which is subject to sickness, decay and death. For the human being, salvation is "becoming what we are," that is, rediscovering our creatureliness.

Salvation is about reconciliation — of persons within themselves, of persons within community, of persons with God and with nature. This vision of salvation is profoundly relational, therefore it presupposes love. It is a process not yet brought to completion, therefore it includes hope. It transcends human experience, therefore it requires faith.

Sin's brokenness extends to nature

Moreover, the brokenness caused by sin extends to nature. The land has fallen under the "curse of sin" and is subject to futility and decay. Indeed, all creation suffers fragmentation and estrangement and longs for freedom from subjugation and exploitation. The biblical image is of a cosmos which groans like a woman in labor, waiting and straining after the moment of deliverance.

The disorder in creation is seen most clearly in the struggle between nature and humanity. At its best, this symbiotic relationship has yielded mutual benefit — human life on earth is enhanced and the land is revitalized. At its worst, however, it has seen the raping of nature and the misuse of its precious elements for weapons of extreme destructiveness.

The splitting of the atom symbolizes the ambiguity of the relationship between humanity and nature. This tiny act of fragmentation leads to the potential for global nuclear annihilation. Human beings have gained a technological ascendancy over nature, but it is not clear whether we have power over this power.

We have spoken of freedom as essential to becoming human, and that freedom is known only in the act of exercising freedom, that is, in choosing to live creatively in the world. It is also obvious that this freedom is not absolute. Humanity is bounded not only by "finitude" — being tied to a particular time and space and always living in the face of death — or by contingency — being limited by choices already made — but also by sinfulness. Sin inevitably distorts our choices and warps our freedom.

Urban T. Holmes provides a helpful perspective on the way in which evil distorts. He speaks of symbols and diabols. The English word "symbol" is rooted in the Greek *sumballo*, meaning "to throw" or "to put together." The Greek word *dia-ballo* means "to slander" or "to mislead," indicating a fragmentation and a pulling apart of what belongs together. It is the root of the English word "diabolical." The diabolical, then, is the power of evil to distort, to lie, to tear asunder.

accordance with the divine "yes" to creation — it is good — and the divine "no" to self-sufficiency — it is not good to be alone.

Human existence is invested with a value that has religious meaning prior to any particular religious institution, tradition or dogma. All life is sacred. Men and women are invested with divine dignity and created for communion. Life itself is a sacrament of divine grace. Social relations, therefore, are ultimately meaningful.

The inescapable reality of sin

Tragically, so much of our experience is of the brokenness, rather than of the wholeness, of life. Not everyone is treated with the same degree of dignity and worth. Life in community is an ongoing struggle between the forces of good and evil, love and hatred, justice and injustice.

There is a deep ambivalence at the personal, interpersonal and social levels of life. Greed, anxiety, despair and restlessness are all signs of the ambiguity of the life described in the Bible as "fallen." Of this struggle the apostle Paul says, "I can will what is right but I cannot do it. For I do not do the good I want, but the evil I do not want is what I do" (Romans 7:18b-19).

Paul then speaks of the sin that dwells within him. The traditional Christian understanding of *sin* holds that it is both personal and impersonal. The shortest and most precise definition of sin in the Bible is found in Romans 14:23: "Whatever does not proceed from faith is sin." Faith is the only way to relate to God. Sin is everything that distorts this relationship, and the tragic consequences of this distortion are seen in history.

Sin has to do with our life together. "What it comes to," says the Apostle James, "is that anyone who knows the right thing to do and does not do it is a sinner" (James 4:17). We are, as Raymond Fung has said, both "sinners and sinned-against." Sin is an inescapable and irresistible reality in our broken world.

Sin ultimately stems from selfishness — the desire of the self for the self. We are tempted by our own desires, and "desire when it has conceived gives birth to sin; and sin when it is full grown brings forth death" (James 1:15). We have been created as free, responsive beings. But the risk of being created with the freedom to feel and to desire is that we can be either life-givers or life-takers. We can share the stuff of life or we can withhold it. Erich Fromm calls this the tension between "being" and "having."

The anxious desire for personal identity and security through what we possess is evidence of a selfish life. It is also self-delusion, described in the Bible by the images of "lostness" and "blindness." Sin, as a distorted way of life, ultimately kills because it cuts us off from the source of life. Without the love of God and the love of our neighbor we are lost and alone. Sin makes us blind to our real self.

Sinfulness in our life together is most evident today where uncritical support is given to the structures that perpetuate social injustice. The lie is that the hierarchical dualisms that divide society belong to the nature of things, that they have an eternal dignity. Even the church has appealed to the "orders of creation" or "natural law" in order to justify the status quo and validate present social arrangements. Such is the subtlety of sin — it can parade with religious dignity and moral conviction through those who believe they are acting according to the "will of God."

Social evil may be overwhelming, but it is not essential. People are still the subjects of history and the creators of social relations. Evils such as racism, sexism and poverty are part of the world that men and women have made for themselves. Behind every injustice stands human responsibility. It may be easier to succumb to the way things are than to resist.

Nonetheless, we are free and responsible beings who cannot afford to hide from the dark side of reality. Many today see the need for a different way of being in the world. Sadly, those who show the courage to resist social evil are often demonized and rejected by society.

How does salvation arrive? We have said that faith is indispensable for becoming truly human, and that faith in the fullest sense of the word includes two referents. On the one hand, faith is necessary for the individual to develop to full maturity. We grow as we learn, and we learn as we place our faith in the faith of others whose lives and commitments we value highly and whose testimony we find meaningful. Faith has a human referent which allows the individual to transcend his or her contingent experience.

On the other hand, faith includes a transcendent dimension, that is, it includes the reality "God." For believers, this transcendent dimension of faith is fundamental to our way of understanding the world, and of preeminent value in shaping our lives in the world. Faith has a divine referent that allows the individual to transcend his or her finite experience.

In both instances, the experience of faith is transmitted through a community of faith, and includes, but is not restricted to, the recognition of exemplars, fidelity to the community's traditions, and participation in the creeds and customs of a particular culture. Salvation is mediated through the life of faith.

The question is how to hold these two aspects of faith together without resorting to the dualistic thinking that so besets our times. To speak of faith in God without reference to humanity is meaningless. To speak of faith in humanity without reference to God is inadequate.

The Exodus story and its implications

Here we run into the problem of language. The dynamics of faith and, therefore, the stuff of salvation cannot be adequately captured in the scientific language of cause and effect. Nor can the efficacy of faith be reduced to the instruments and applications of technique. The language most appropriate to the life of faith is sacramental, and the language of sacrament is the language of "story."

With images, metaphors and symbols, through narrative, song and dramatic action, the faith of the community is recalled, expressed, celebrated, energized and carried forward. Interpreters of the Judeo-Christian story of faith speak of a "salvation history" in which history and eternity, immanence and transcendence, humanity and divinity are intertwined into one grand cosmic drama.

The biblical narrative is replete with dynamic images through which the writers tell of the "mighty acts of God" by which a people are formed and transformed. The Exodus narrative is a prime example of this interface between the "acts of God" and the faith development of the people of Israel.

The story tells us of God's action through Moses to deliver a dispirited and destitute people from their slavery in Egypt and of their subsequent formation into a covenant community. The narrative text contains the potent historical memory of the people's liberation and salvation. Through the repeated recitation and reenactment of this memory in the life of the community this liberation story prompts, prods and provokes the people of God into renewed faith and appropriate actions.

In this way, says Walter Brueggemann, "the community appropriates its normative memory and its governing metaphors" in a process that is "not only recollective but also formative." Each generation is exposed to the "peculiar angle of vision" that the Exodus narrates. Not only the original event, but the narrative of the event and the continuing impact of the narrative text in the life of the community mediates the saving efficacy of God's activity from generation to generation.

God as the Saving One

There is a powerful simplicity in the Exodus story. The people cry out in their pain. God hears their cry and is moved to action. Life begins for the nation of Israel. Exodus, the Covenant at Sinai, and the settlement in the Promised Land are the originating events of a faith that confesses and celebrates God as the Saving One. Salvation — health, healing and wholeness — comes from God's side.

Moreover, the experience of salvation is, at the same time, the revelation of a God who creates "something out of nothing." In this particular revelation of God in creating a new life and identity arises the confession that God is indeed the Creator of all that is. Against the background of this particular historical event, Israel's faith reaches out to embrace all of history: creation "in the beginning" (Gen. 1:1), and new creation at the end in "the new heavens and the new earth" (Isaiah 65:17).

God is worshipped as the universal God who creates and redeems the whole world. As God sees the affliction and hears the groaning of the children of Israel, so God sees, hears and feels the pain and suffering of all creation.

The Exodus event, and the impact of this event on the life of Israel as recorded in the biblical narrative, has profound implications for our understanding of health, healing and wholeness. First, evil, as manifested in the dominant and oppressive systems and structures of the world, is not to be blindly obeyed or passively endured. Healing begins when the oppressed public protests against its plight and refuses to acknowledge any longer the right of the ruling elite to dominate, divide and destroy.

God hears the cries of the poor and acts for their deliverance. God is on their side. The presence of social divisions in the covenant community is an abrogation of God's standards of justice. The "holiness" of the people of God is measured by the "wholeness" of their social practices. God wills to heal the brokenness of the people.

Second, pain, the raw edge of physical, mental, social and spiritual suffering, must be given voice. Pain of itself is not the enemy. Pain warns of the presence of disease, distress and destruction. The healthy organism needs the facility of pain to remain healthy. Pain is a necessary element in the healing process. Simply deadening the pain does not constitute healing.

Silencing the voices of those who suffer, or blaming the victim, is a deadly subterfuge for dealing with the presence of social disorder. The perpetration of the social evils of discrimination and domination for the good pleasure of the elite, and the perpetuation of pain and suffering in the face of the cries of the people, is an abomination which moves the heart of God.

The reality of the kingdom of God

When protest over the destructiveness of sin and evil finds its expression in the public processing of pain, which in the Bible is captured most eloquently in the songs, litanies, poems and prophetic speeches of the hurting community, then new possibilities emerge for an alternative future beyond the brokenness and fragmentation. This is the dimension of hope that pervades the Old and New Testament alike.

Hope dreams alternative realities and constructs new social arrangements in keeping with this new and still future reality. Hope creates an open space within which the process of healing toward health and wholeness, which are eschatological realities, can take place. Hope is the womb out of which the future is born through pain and with resistance.

The primary metaphor in the Bible for this new social reality is the *kingdom of God*. The "kingdom" metaphor speaks of a realm of authority and a domain in which this authority is recognized in the everyday arrangements of life. It is a manifestly public and political notion. But this "kingdom" is not just any kingdom — it is the kingdom of God. That is to say, it is the realm in which the sovereignty of God is recognized and celebrated.

This kingdom is not created by extending the present social, political and economic arrangements, or through the ingenuity of human imagination, or by extrapolating from human experience. Rather, it is "given" by God, revealed through faith and entered by grace.

The kingdom of God is that realm in which the salvation of God is made effective for all creation. Since all creation, animate and inanimate, still groans under the weight of evil and still suffers from the diabolical fragmentation of life, it is evident that the kingdom of God is yet to be revealed in all its fullness.

The kingdom is a future reality, that is, in terms of human history God is yet to be recognized as "all and in all." And yet the kingdom is present. It is present in the moments of healing grace, wherever people embrace the salvation of God and experience the liberation of faith. It is present wherever the powers of evil are being exposed and challenged. It is present wherever people receive and live out of the promise of God for a new future.

The journey thus far

Let us review the journey we have taken thus far. I began with the observation that present-day reality is circumscribed by deep divisions at all levels of existence. Moreover, these divisions are but the outward manifestation of our dualistic way of thinking, especially in the Western world. Life is ordered into dominant and inferior entities, powerful and powerless groups. Such hierarchical dualisms abound and are evidence of the skewing, even the breaking, of relationships.

Fragmentation, rather than wholeness, is the customary experience of life. Society is seized by an endemic sickness. I have portrayed this sickness in terms of the "diabolical," separating that which belongs together, and as "sin," to indicate the fundamental and willful break in relationship between humanity and God, between the creature and the Creator.

Health, healing and wholeness has to do with discovering the means and the conditions by which broken human beings can become "truly human." I have suggested that this is not possible without the restoration of relationships at all levels of life, and the discovery of a foundation upon which these relationships can be established. To this end I have suggested that the Judeo-Christian vision of the God of creation and redemption, as portrayed in the scriptures, reveals a way by which life can be reconstructed. Such "reconstruction" in the midst of life is the experience of "salvation."

Salvation comes from God. God alone can save us, for we are too deeply immersed in the morass of sin to extricate ourselves from its power. God takes the initiative and moves toward us. God meets us at the point of our need — as sinners in need of forgiveness, as enemies in need of reconciliation. God arrives to tell us what we cannot tell ourselves: "You are loved! You are accepted! You are free!"

Becoming a new creation

God *is* love. God in his love is *for us*. God is for us as the lover is for the beloved. To experience the love of God is to find a meaning which "centers" our existence. In this relationship we become a "new creation." Our lives are now determined by the God whose passion it is to restore all life and to bring it to fulfillment.

This has consequences for our lives. First, as God *is* for us, so we can *be* for others. This opens up a whole new way of living, or a new way of living wholesomely. Second, our experience of personal salvation fosters within us the hope and longing for the salvation of everything and everyone. We are started on the journey toward the horizon of full salvation — the promised fulfillment in the kingdom of God. On the way, we are called into partnership with God as co-creators of the future.

The journey toward wholeness includes pain and suffering. These are not realities which can be left behind, regardless of what the prophets of health in our culture may tell us. Health is not simply the absence of illness. If health were the absence of illness, then the sick and the handicapped and the frail would be defined out of the good society. This is clearly unacceptable, but never far away in our Western way of thinking.

Health is a relative, rather than an absolute, condition. Since reality has been defined in relational terms, health language can no longer appeal to absolutes. Relationships involve partnerships, and in genuine relationships the "other" in the partnership is never under our control. Therefore, the appropriate attitude is vulnerability and openness.

We do not take the journey alone. We have examples to inspire us. The writer to the Hebrew Christians spoke of the great heroes of the Judeo-Christian tradition, those men and women of faith who allowed their lives to be shaped by the promises of God. They are our "great cloud of witnesses" whose lives are a shining example of investing in the right cause. "Therefore, since we are surrounded by so great a cloud of witnesses," says the writer, "let us also lay aside every weight and sin which clings so closely..." (Heb. 12:1a).

We not only have examples to live by, we have a Savior to follow. "In these last days," says the writer to the Hebrews, "God has spoken to us by a Son" (Heb. 1:2). Of this conviction the New Testament writers are of one voice — that in Jesus of Nazareth we have the definitive self-communication of God.

God is revealed in Jesus Christ, that is, God has become one with us in our humanity. Since God has shared the divine life with the man Jesus, we must now understand God on the basis of the life and destiny of this man. This means we cannot construct God in our image to justify our own interests and validate the status quo. Since the cross is the key to understanding the life of Jesus we can say that God shares his life with broken humanity, and accepts the deadly consequences of this identification.

Resurrection declares that death does not have the final word. In following God in Christ we become the servants of life. The corresponding life style is "discipleship." Therefore, concludes the writer to the Hebrews, "let us run with perseverance the race that is set before us, looking to Jesus, the pioneer and perfecter of our faith, who for the joy that was set before him endured the cross, despising the shame, and is seated at the right hand of the throne of God" (Heb. 12:1b-2).

DISCIPLESHIP FOR TRANSFORMATION

Jesus stepped out of obscurity in the insignificant village of Nazareth to announce the momentous news that God was about to do a new thing in Israel. "The time is fulfilled," Jesus said. "The kingly rule of God has drawn near; repent and believe the good news" (Mark 1:14-15).

God's reign of grace had begun to break into human history. What is more, Jesus interpreted his own calling in terms of the arrival of the kingdom. "The Spirit of the Lord is upon me, because he has anointed me to proclaim release for the captives and recovery of sight for the blind, to set at liberty those who are oppressed, to proclaim the acceptable year of the Lord" (Luke 4:18-19).

The idea of the kingdom of God was a central element of the political, social and religious tradition of Israel. From the earliest days they had celebrated the kingly presence of God in their festivals and worship. They understood themselves to be a "kingdom of priests and a holy nation" (Exodus 19:6), and looked to the Temple and the Torah to enable them to fulfill the requirements of the covenant.

But the people of Israel had fallen upon hard times. Reality was no longer in accord with their kingdom rhetoric. A succession of Davidic kings had failed to measure up to standard as the instruments of God. Conquest and dominance by foreign powers had shattered their confidence in the present.

God's kingdom went underground and was kept alive in the hopes and dreams of a captive people that one day God's word would be vindicated, and God's people would be set free. Specifically, they hoped for either a restoration of the Davidic kingdom in an Israel free of Roman occupation or an apocalyptic universal kingdom of God with Jerusalem and its Temple at the center.

Jesus proclaims the day of salvation

Jesus boldly announced that the day of salvation had arrived. The power of evil had been overcome, and the prince of evil had been toppled (Luke 10:18). The salvation of God's kingdom is present and available. The future "wholeness" can be experienced now.

He invited the skeptics in his hearing to examine the evidence — demons being cast out (Luke 11:20), the blind seeing, the lame walking, lepers being cleansed, the deaf hearing, the dead being raised, and the Good News was preached to the poor (Luke 7:22).

In the name of God, Jesus healed the sick, forgave sinners and embraced the poor, the persecuted and the pitied with such familiarity that no one could mistake the implication that God was at home with them. Unlike apocalyptic prophets such as John the Baptist, who lived the life of an ascetic and whose disciples fasted, Jesus and his disciples were accused of being gluttons and drunkards who kept company with tax collectors and sinners (Mark 2:18ff, Luke 7:34).

The kingdom of God, Jesus said, is like a glorious banquet, a wedding feast. All are invited and all are welcome. The invitation, however, has to be accepted. But the powerful were blind to the significance of the invitation. They were being offered a way into the presence of God but were insulted by the presence of the poor. Yes, the day had arrived, but it was surely veiled.

In parable, preaching and personal demonstration, Jesus taught that the kingdom of God is a realm to be entered by faith, not a regime that will be imposed by force. The touchstone of this kingdom is grace. God is offering the gift of life. This gift can be discovered at any moment, as a treasure too great to be overlooked, as an invitation too wonderful to be rejected.

Grace is to be discovered in the world around us, and, in keeping with its nature as surprise, in the least likely of people and places. Since it is a gift, it requires acceptance without hesitation. Yet when all is said and done, it is costly — it will cost us all we have and all we are. The gift of grace seeks no less than a radical reorientation of life.

Jesus called people to a new life style based on the values of the kingdom of God. This new life begins with repentance. Repentance, according to Jesus, is more than just feeling remorse for your sins. It is a decision which involves a radical renunciation of evil and a resolute turning towards God.

It issues in a life of faith, where faith is understood not as the rational acceptance of certain dogmatic propositions, but as a radical openness to the gracious presence and leading of God in community. In the Gospels, the life of repentance and faith is presented as the life of *discipleship* — the unconditional response of a person to the unconditional demand of Jesus to "Follow me!" (Mark 1:17).

Jesus' command to "follow me" is the characteristic call to discipleship in the Gospels. The sense throughout is one of movement. Jesus is "passing by," or "going a little further" when he calls the person directly to follow him. The disciple joins Jesus "on the way," the way being "the way to Jerusalem and the cross."

Henceforth, disciples are known as the *followers* of Jesus, not just in the narrow sense of *imitating* him, as is the case with any exemplar, but in the fuller sense of *identifying* with him in the nature and purpose of the journey, and dependence upon him as the leader. We follow Jesus as "the way, the truth and the life" (John 14:6).

The journey with Jesus leads to the cross, and beyond that into the resurrection life of the risen Christ in and through the community of faith. As Lord, Jesus leads the disciple band on the journey. As Savior, Jesus opens up the way to the future.

Miscalculating the cost

The journey of faith is not easy, nor the pathway always clear. This is to be expected, for the journey is *toward* wholeness and full maturity. The disciple does not set out on the journey of faith with a perfect holiness. Obedience is learned "on the way," by struggling through the ambivalence that is a part and parcel of "not knowing in full."

Miscalculating the cost and misunderstanding the nature of discipleship are intrinsic to the journey. The notion that the disciple sets out on this journey with an absolute certainty of the way, and with the security of having the holiness issue settled in advance, is a fallacy which is refuted by both the witness of scripture and the testimony of our own ambiguous attempts to follow Christ.

There is abroad today a form of Christianity that promotes a so-called "theology of success" which brooks no contradiction. Admissions of doubt, uncertainty, struggle and failure are condemned as signs of "bad faith." Such arrant, even arrogant, fundamentalism is out of step with the life of faith depicted in the Bible and beautifully captured in the confession "I believe; help my unbelief!" (Mark 9:24)

Consider once more the Exodus story. Having been delivered from the pain, drudgery and ignominy of slavery in Egypt, the children of Israel set out on a journey toward the Promised Land. But the journey was long and they grew tired. Even the food that Yahweh supplied in abundance began to taste familiar and old. They began to grumble as their impatience grew.

They spoke against God and Moses, saying, "Why have you brought us up out of Egypt to die in the wilderness?" (Numbers 21:5). Israel was free, but not fully free. They had replaced the fear and tyranny of the known with the fear and tyranny of the unknown. The journey was long and hard, and they wanted to go back.

God heard their cry. But this time God sent fiery snakes among the people so that many were bitten and many died. Then the people turned to Moses and confessed their failure, and Moses interceded with God on their behalf. God commanded Moses to make a bronze serpent and set it on a pole so that whenever someone was bitten they could look at the bronze serpent and be healed. The image of the bronze serpent here serves as a symbol for Yahweh's power to heal and to forgive.

The Gospel of Mark and discipleship

It is to the Gospel of St. Mark that I now want to turn to explicate the meaning of "discipleship" in light of the ambivalence of faith evident in the journey of experience of the first disciples.

It should be noted from the outset that Mark is addressing a particular audience, presumably a community with which he is familiar, and whose needs are uppermost in his mind as he constructs his Gospel. While scholars are not agreed on the precise details of Mark's community, we know that it is a post-resurrection community, almost certainly in Rome. We can infer that the question, "What does it mean to be a disciple of Jesus?" is an issue for this community.

Mark's Gospel is a carefully crafted answer to this pastoral concern. He has selected and arranged his material in such a way that a compelling picture emerges of Jesus: "The Son of Man did not come to be served but to serve, and to give his life as a ransom for many" (Mark 10:45); and of the disciples, "Whoever would be great among you must be your servant" (Mark 10:43).

Mark's major treatment of discipleship is found in the great central section of his Gospel, chapters 8:22-10:52. The section begins and ends with the healing of blind men. It begins with the healing of a blind man that requires two attempts. It finishes with the healing of blind Bartimaeus, who then immediately follows Jesus on the way to Jerusalem. These two healings not only give the frame for the section of teaching on discipleship, they also indicate the type of picture we are dealing with.

The reference to "blindness" alerts us to the deeper meaning of this section. "Blindness" carries a double meaning. On the one hand, blindness refers to a physical condition that requires healing for sight to be restored. Jesus is the one who makes the blind to see. On the other hand, blindness refers to a lack of spiritual insight.

Restoration of sight is a metaphor for spiritual understanding. In the passage preceding this section, Mark stresses the hardness of heart and the blindness of the disciples in the face of Jesus' feeding of the five thousand (Mark 8:14-21). Here is a clue for understanding what is to follow.

The section we are examining is cast in the form of a journey to Jerusalem. The journey falls roughly into three parts. Each begins with a prediction by Jesus of his impending suffering, death and resurrection. On each occasion the disciples fail to understand the significance of Jesus' suffering, death and resurrection for their lives. Their attitudes, reflected in their subsequent conduct, reveal their lack of understanding of what it means to be a disciple of Jesus.

Then follows teaching by Jesus on the nature of true discipleship. We notice immediately that discipleship is placed in the light of the cross and resurrection. The life of Jesus and the life of the disciple go hand in hand.

Who is Jesus?

The first part (8:27-9:29) begins with Jesus asking the disciples to share with him the people's speculation as to his identity. They tell him that some say "John the Baptist," that is to say that the reality that has come to life in Jesus is the same reality which inspired John. But John came preaching a message of repentance based on the requirements of the law and in the light of the apocalyptic judgment which was to come. Jesus preached the reign of God as a time of grace and acceptance for the sinner, and that its time had now begun. This answer is clearly inadequate.

"Others say, Elijah," they add; "and others one of the prophets." But unlike Elijah, Jesus was not a guardian of the religious traditions of Israel, and while some of the elements of the prophets are clearly visible in Jesus they do not account for his unique ministry.

Then Jesus directs the question away from popular speculation and asks, "Who do you say that I am?" What role does Jesus play in their existence? Peter responds on behalf of the disciples, "You are the Christ!" Peter risks new language to try and express his conviction that Jesus is more than a prophet, that he is the "Anointed One" through whom God will save the people. It was, and is, the archetypal confession of orthodoxy.

Jesus does not uncritically accept the title of Messiah. In his ministry he had gone way beyond the parameters expected of the Messiah of God in Jewish expectation. He had broken the law, dispensed forgiveness for sins, and shared table fellowship with tax collectors, publicans, outcasts and sinners. Jesus responds to Peter's confession by speaking of his coming suffering, rejection, death and resurrection. This he says plainly, addressing the people.

Peter is not about to have the agenda of the Messiah changed from glorious liberator to suffering servant. He rebukes Jesus. Peter allows his self-interest to intrude upon his confession of faith, bending his orthodoxy to heresy. Peter uses his confession as a shield with which to fend off Jesus' idea of suffering as a revelation of the divine intention.

Peter attempts to correct Jesus in the name, and for the best interests, of God. No wonder Jesus' response locates Peter's confession on the side of the demonic: "Get behind me, Satan!" Peter wants Jesus to be Lord, but will not allow Jesus to fill the content of this "Lordship." Peter's confession is only half-way there.

In other words, Peter is half-sighted and needs a second touch. Full sight will come only upon a full acceptance and understanding of the purpose of Jesus. Peter knows that salvation lies with Jesus, but Peter must be prepared to accept the way in which salvation will come, and to shape his discipleship accordingly.

Discipleship and the cross are inseparable

Jesus then teaches his disciples and the crowd the true nature of discipleship. Would-be disciples are to take up their crosses, deny themselves and come after him (8:34). Discipleship and the cross are inseparable. To "take up" the cross is to actively embrace vulnerability, suffering and endurance for the sake of the gospel, that is, for the sake of the new relationship into which God is calling the world.

The disciple is to step into the place of resistance to the gods that dominate this broken world. The disciple is to stand in and with the people who carry the burden of the world's sad divisions — the poor, the broken, the despised, the old, the outsider. To do this requires a new identity at the core of existence.

The disciples are to "deny" themselves, that is, they are to lay down, they are to "lose" their self-constructed identity and to embrace the new identity of being formed by the same Spirit that was in Jesus. It is by attachment to Jesus that the disciple "finds" and "saves" his or her life. The disciple becomes a follower of Jesus, not as one would follow an ethical example, or an ideal, but as one receives a Savior.

The first part concludes with two incidents. The first is the transfiguration of Jesus and the divine voice of approval spoken over Jesus. God legitimizes Jesus as "Son," and validates his teaching on the nature of true discipleship. The disciples are charged to "listen to him."

The second incident concerns the boy who was brought to Jesus' disciples by his father in hopes of being healed. The disciples try, but fail. Jesus successfully heals the boy and then instructs the disciples that prayer is a constitutive element of discipleship.

The second part begins with a further prediction of Jesus' suffering, death and resurrection (9:30-32), followed by the misunderstanding of the disciples as shown by their preoccupation with who was the greatest, and includes a further development in Jesus' teaching on the true meaning of discipleship (9:33-10:31).

The emphasis moves from the disciples' relationship with Jesus to their relations among themselves. Jesus has taught them of the necessity of suffering for the healing of relationships, and they are busy jockeying for positions of leadership and power among their own company.

To demonstrate the appropriate attitude for the disciple, Jesus sets a child in their midst and says, "Whoever receives one such child in my name receives me" (9:37). Jesus inverts the world's power arrangements to demonstrate the way the community of disciples should live. It is the "little ones," the unimportant ones, who are to have preeminence of place and respect, for Jesus identifies himself with them. Greatness is measured by the grace and humility of exalting others, especially those whom society despises or overlooks.

True greatness comes from serving others

We can move to the third prediction and the final part of this section on discipleship. Once again, Mark employs the same pattern of Jesus' prediction of his suffering, death and resurrection, the misunderstanding of the disciples, and Jesus' teaching on the true nature of discipleship. On this occasion, the nature of preeminence among the disciples is taken one step further as James and John come to Jesus asking for the chief portfolios in the kingdom when it is established (10:35-37).

Jesus teaches the disciples once more that true greatness does not come through the exercise of authority, even if it is done in the spirit of humility. On the contrary, it is in serving others, as one who waits on others at a meal, that the disciple finds meaning in life.

The disciple is one who is sensitive and responsive to the everyday needs of others, especially those who are usually overlooked in the course of events. In fulfilling such a ministry, the disciple is doing nothing other than what Jesus did in his own life. And it will be costly. Jesus' life is a reminder that the way of service in the cause of the powerless is a road to suffering and death.

The section closes with the healing of blind Bartimaeus (10:46-52). This blind beggar cries out to Jesus for mercy. The crowd tries to silence his cries, but Bartimaeus will not be silenced for he hopes that in this one who is passing by is to be found the healing for which he longs. He is physically blind, but spiritually he sees what the crowd accompanying Jesus overlooks.

He cries out all the louder. Jesus hears Bartimaeus and asks him what it is that he wants him to do. "Master, let me receive my sight," is the blind beggar's request. Jesus says to him, "Go your way; your faith has made you well" (10:52). Mark employs a specific Greek word which carries a double meaning. Jesus tells Bartimaeus that his faith has both saved and healed him. In return, Bartimaeus immediately follows Jesus on the way.

Let us return to the healing with which Mark begins this section of his gospel — the incomplete healing of the blind man. Given the difficulty with which the first disciples struggled to understand Jesus' teaching on discipleship, a difficulty that Mark's community would surely identify with even as we identify with the first disciples today, Mark's positioning of this healing miracle carries a strong message: how hard it is to open the eyes of the blind. How hard it is for the disciples to understand.

Yet Bartimaeus, destitute in his physical blindness, understands that in Jesus is to be found the answer to his problem. In simple faith he reaches out to Jesus, and in immediate obedience he starts on the road to discipleship. Bartimaeus becomes the epitome of Christian discipleship. Bartimaeus shows us the way to health, healing and wholeness.

Discipleship is following Jesus

Discipleship, therefore, is nothing other and nothing less than following Jesus. The implication of this statement is that the determining reality in Jesus' life and ministry will be the determining reality of the life of the disciple.

What was Jesus' understanding of reality? Without a doubt, Jesus lived out of an awareness of God as a living, loving and liberating reality whose heart is for those whose existence is breaking or is broken. The passion of God for the well-being of people was evident in the formation of the covenant community. As a Jew, Jesus understood that the covenant required the concrete caring of people for each other, and that the efficacy of the covenant was to extend to all nations and to nature itself.

The touchstone of the divine love expressed in the covenant was "justice." Justice involved the protection of the weakest in society. To neglect the weakest and the most vulnerable in the community was to act against the spirit and demands of justice, thereby undermining the well-being of society and denying the efficacy of God's love.

Jesus' whole life was lived out as an embodiment, an incarnation, of the love of God — a love which seeks to restore human dignity where it is marred, to heal that which is broken, and to save that which is lost. Jesus died as a consequence of the way in which he lived. His death on the cross was no accident.

Jesus blessed the poor and proclaimed their day of liberation. In the name of God he forgave sinners, embraced the unclean, shared table fellowship with tax collectors and publicans, and preached that prostitutes would enter the kingdom of God before the priests and politicians. He overturned the interests of those who held economic, political and religious power. Anyone who dared to suggest that the poor may not be poor because of their own fault, but rather because of the injustice of the systems and structures which support the rich, has to die.

Moreover, there was legal foundation in the Torah for Jesus to be put to death. According to Leviticus 24:16, "He who blasphemes the name of the Lord shall be put to death." Jesus was condemned as a blasphemer and was delivered to the Romans to be crucified. Jesus' death satisfied the demands of "holiness" according to the Torah, and was in keeping with the "will of God" according to the cult.

When the disciples finally understood what Jesus had been telling them all along would happen, they fled. Only the women in the disciple band remained. In the silence that accompanied the death of Jesus on Good Friday, it appeared that the Pharisees were vindicated in their role as guardians of the purity of God.

But Christians confess that the final word had yet to be spoken. In the resurrection of Jesus from the dead, God spoke a new and decisive word. God, who shared the divine life with Jesus, raised this same Jesus to life again, thereby validating Jesus' view of reality.

The cross, therefore, is not the end of the journey. Jesus continues to lead the disciple band. It is the presence of the living Lord that makes the journey possible and endurable. The cross is not negated, nor left behind. Rather, whenever the disciples invest their lives in the same things in which Jesus invested his, the cross becomes the symbol of their destiny. The powers of destruction are still in evidence, and the keepers of the status quo still defend their positions with awesome power. The disciple is not to be naive about the reality and depth of evil in society.

The resurrection stands as the symbol of the hope that God will keep faith with the disciple band in the same way in which God kept faith with the crucified Jesus. This hope has a sure foundation, for the death of Jesus had a profound impact on God. God was exposed to death. God took the sting of death and robbed it of its power forever.

To be a disciple, then, is to stake our lives on the things for which Jesus lived. Concretely, this means accepting outcasts and infidels, forgiving enemies and welcoming strangers. It means living out of the awareness that God is present in the world today as healing and restoring love. As we receive the grace of God, the grace which bestows identity and restores our dignity, so we are to mediate that love to others.

It also means a reversal of commonly held values — the first shall be last, the least shall be the greatest, the one who will lead must serve. Life is gained not by grasping it, but by giving it away. These are the values of the kingdom of God that Jesus brought to life.

Being a disciple, therefore, is responding to the call of Jesus to leave behind the old way of life and follow him on the road. The road leads to the future salvation and restoration of all things. The prophet Isaiah dreams of this time as the creation of a "new heaven and a new earth." In this new creation, peace, *shalom*, well-being will be enjoyed by all.

The field and the earth will bring forth abundance. The yoke of oppression will be no more, and hurt and destruction will not be remembered. There will be an overwhelming joy in the hearts of the people — they will rejoice with exceeding delight. There shall be no more tears, no more premature deaths, no more infant mortality. There will be a new economic order in which none shall usurp the goods of another and everyone shall be adequately fed, clothed and housed (Isaiah 65:17-25).

In the meantime, the community of disciples gathered around Jesus is to create analogies to the kingdom of God in their common life in the world. In this way will God's kingdom come and God's will be done on earth as it is in heaven.

Discipleship is a powerful source of healing in a world characterized by brokenness at all levels of life. It is powerful because it recognizes that a fundamental change in values and life style is essential to effect the kind of healing needed in a fragmented world, and it proposes a viable alternative to the isolation and alienation that results from such fragmentation.

Fundamental to the life of discipleship is the formation of community which, despite all its ambiguities in a less than perfect world, still provides a model for developing health and healing relationships — with God, with others, and with nature.

Jacob's limp as a paradigm for ministry

Finally, there is no guarantee that the healers will not be wounded in the process of living the life of discipleship. I have already made reference to the type of Christianity that seeks to avoid vulnerability and pain. Let me suggest one closing image for what I believe is a more appropriate ministry paradigm for the church — the paradigm of Jacob's limp.

I have suggested that the brokenness of life is manifest in the brokenness of relationships. By the same token, salvation as health, healing and wholeness is to be found in the restoration of relationships.

The book of Genesis provides us with a moving account of the reconciliation between two brothers whose enmity was long and deep (Gen. 32-33). Esau sells his birthright to his brother Jacob for a hearty meal. Jacob gains by deception the blessing due to Esau from their dying father.

From the outset the family is divided in its loyalties. Jacob flees to avoid the danger of his brother's anger. But the time comes, as it inevitably does, when the brothers have to meet face to face. God calls Jacob to return to his home country and promises to be with him for his protection. God purposes to honor his promise to Abraham and Isaac to make of their descendants a mighty nation.

Jacob is afraid. He makes the necessary preparations to placate his brother's anger. On the night before their meeting, Jacob remains alone to pray to God for a blessing. The story tells us that Jacob "wrestled with a man until the breaking of the day. When the man saw that he did not prevail against Jacob, he touched the hollow of his thigh; and Jacob's thigh was put out of joint" (Gen. 32:24-25).

Jacob refuses to let the man go until he receives the blessing he seeks. The man asks him, "What is your name?" And he replies, "Jacob." Then the man says, "Your name shall no more be called Jacob, but Israel, for you have striven with God and with men and have prevailed" (Gen. 32:28).

Jacob receives the blessing he sought from God. But he still has to meet his brother whom he had wronged, and whose response he can neither predict nor control. Jacob is blessed, but he is not excused from the pain, anxiety and vulnerability of reconciling with his brother.

Much to Jacob's surprise, Esau runs to meet him. He embraces him and kisses him. And in the joy and release of that embrace which heals, they weep. The broken past is dealt with, and a future opened up. But notice that Esau did what Jacob could not do: he ran. Jacob could only limp. He could neither run to nor from his brother, or from anyone else for that matter. He had walked away from his meeting with God with three things — with God's blessing for his protection and his future, with a new name, and with a permanent limp.

The deep healing required in Jacob's world of relationships included the reality "God." Jacob received the blessing of God's salvation, but at a cost. The healing that deals with relationships and values includes breaking, wounding, and even permanent scars. This is what Jesus implied when he said to his disciples that unless a grain of wheat falls into the ground and is broken open it will not live again to produce much more grain (John 12:24). Would-be healers are not spared from being wounded.

But we are not alone. God in Christ was, and is, no stranger to the pain required of healing. For the sake of healing a broken creation, God suffered the pain and death of the beloved Son. The Son suffered the pain and humiliation of the cross, and as the Risen One still bears the scars of crucifixion. Isaiah's vision of the Suffering Servant is applicable:

> *Surely he has borne our griefs*
> *and carried our sorrows;*
> *yet we esteemed him stricken,*
> *smitten by God, and afflicted.*
> *But he was wounded for our transgressions,*
> *he was bruised for our iniquities;*
> *upon him was the chastisement that makes us whole,*
> *and with his stripes we are healed.*
> Isaiah 53:4-5

Jacob, we are told, is "Israel." The church, we are told, is the "New Israel." May it be that Jacob's limp becomes the paradigm of Christian ministry in the world. Only in this way will the church fulfill her calling to be the humble disciples of Jesus Christ, and the agents of God's powerful healing in and for the world.

Selected Bibliography

BEST, Ernest. *Following Jesus: Discipleship in the Gospel of Mark.* Sheffield: JSOT Press, 1981.

BRUEGGEMANN, Walter. *Hope Within History.* Atlanta: John Knox Press, 1987.

FIORENZA, Elisabeth Schuessler. *In Memory of Her: A Feminist Theological Reconstruction of Christian Origins.* London: SCM Press, 1983.

GILKEY, Langdon. *Reaping the Whirlwind: A Christian Interpretation of History.* New York: The Seabury Press, 1976.

GILL, Athol. *Life on the Road: The Gospel Basis for a Messianic Lifestyle.* Sydney: Anzea Publishers, 1989.

HOLMES, Urban T. III. *Ministry and Imagination.* New York: The Seabury Press, 1976.

McFAGUE, Sallie. *Models of God: Theology for an Ecological, Nuclear Age.* Philadelphia: Fortress Press, 1987.

MOLTMANN, Juergen. *God in Creation: An Ecological Doctrine of Creation.* London: SCM Press, 1985.

SEGUNDO, Juan Luis. *Faith and Ideologies.* New York: Orbis Books, Maryknoll, 1984.

TILLICH, Paul. "The Relation of Religion and Health," in *Healing: Human and Divine,* ed. Simon Doniger. New York: Association Press, 1957.

THREE

EGYPT TO ISRAEL: HEALTHCARE AND SUSTAINABLE DEVELOPMENT

Bryant L. Myers

EGYPT TO ISRAEL: THE STORY

The People of Israel in Egypt

*They would not listen to him
because their spirit had been
broken by their cruel slavery.
Exodus 6:9*

The People of Israel in the Desert

*We felt as small as
grasshoppers, and that is
how we must
have looked to them.
Numbers 13:33*

The People of God at the Edge of the Jordan

*We will do everything you
have told us and will go
anywhere you send us.
Joshua 1:16*

It took a matter of days to get Israel out of Egypt; it took 40 years in the wilderness to get Egypt out of Israel. This reflection will examine the pilgrimage of the people of Israel from Egypt to Israel in terms of making the development process possible. Three questions will be asked and then the relationship will be applied to sustainable healthcare.

- What was the difference between the community of faith as it was in Egypt and as it was on the edge of the Jordan, just prior to entering into the Promised Land?

- What enabled this change to take place? What got in the way?

- What lessons can we learn for enabling development to take place today?

What were the people of Israel like in Egypt, and what did they become as a result of their desert experience? How can we contrast the two?

In Egypt	*In Israel*
Not a people; not a group with a sense of self-identity; broken of spirit; brickmakers	A nation, a chosen people; a people who knew who they were and where they were going
Building someone else's country, working for someone else's future	Building their own country; working toward their own future
A broken society with a broken spirit; limited social structure; in need of care	A whole society with a social and religious structure, caring for its widows, orphans and foreigners
A people with no future, facing brickmaking without straw and officially sanctioned genocide	A people with an exciting future as a nation; with a mission to be a blessing to others
A people whose spirits were full of fear, who looked back when the going got tough	A people who thought they could do anything; who worked toward an unseen, promised future

From being a group with a broken spirit, facing the death of their first-born sons, to a nation looking forward with a purpose; from being needy foreigners in someone else's land to caring for foreigners in their own land; from fearful people who felt small and inadequate and always found reasons for saying, "we can't do it," to people who no longer saw giants in the land — what a transformation. Truly this is liberation!

What made possible this development, this transformation?

Because we are a people of the Book, this is also our story. What can we learn from this story?

First and foremost, they came to know and to trust a God who was with them — a God who spoke, who communicated, who led them and provided for them. Walking with this God through the desert transformed their view of themselves and their world.

As Christians, we have the one critical success factor to human and community development that no secular agency has — the Good News, the whole gospel. The Good News to the poor is that they too have a God who cares, a God who can be known, a God who hears their cry and feels their pain, and a God who insists on a better future for them. The minute we forget or underplay the importance of our evangelism strategy in our development work, we set aside the greatest contribution we have to share.

Second, they had a leader who listened to God. Moses was a critical factor in reminding the people of what their God required. The importance of local leadership, especially local Christian leaders, can make or break the development process.

Third, they were taught skills that allowed them to survive in the desert. They learned that a certain kind of wood took away the bitterness in undrinkable water. They learned to fight battles and win them. They learned to use a census to plan and to organize. They learned how to deal with lepers and sanitation. They were taught to become competent as a people.

Fourth, God gave them a priesthood and the Law. The religious dimension of life was developed. But this new religious structure was much more than a way to meet interior spiritual needs. It was also the means by which God began to develop the kingdom ethics and values of the community; the vision of life together that could make a just people, a people whose very rules of living together prevented any from creating or sustaining poverty.

Fifth, God gave them beauty in the form of sacramental art. In Exodus 31 we read that, "The Lord said to Moses, 'I have chosen Bezalel, the son of Uri and the grandson of Hur, from the tribe of Judah, and I have filled him with my power. I have given him the understanding, skill and ability for every kind of artistic work.'"

This is the first time in the Bible we learn of God gifting people. Brickmakers and herdsmen, broken and feeling without value, need culture, beauty and art. They need to be able to see things that are theirs that are beautiful and worthy of praise. This is part of the process of developing a feeling that things may not need to continue as they always have been: perhaps we do have value; perhaps the future can be different.

Finally, God, through Moses, developed a social structure. Extended poverty and oppression breaks down and distorts the structure and social fabric of a community. These destructive or debilitating changes need to be overcome. Under Moses, judges were given delegated responsibility — the camp was organized, the priesthood was set apart, the responsibility for caring for the widow, the orphan and the foreigner was established. For an oppressed people to become a transformed community, they must develop the internal social structures and rules by which they can create and transform both themselves and their community.

This is an interesting list: getting to know God; having a leader who listens to God; learning skills; developing an enhanced religious structure focused on community ethics; adding beauty and culture; and transforming the social structure.

It is important to note that only two of the six can be provided from outside the community. Evangelism can introduce people to a God they have not met. A skilled facilitator can help people learn new skills. But the rest — leadership, quality of community life, art and culture, and a transformed social structure — must all emerge from within. There appears to be a limit to what intervention from outside the community can do. And even with God's intervention, it took 40 years.

What factors hindered the development process?

Let's look at the other side of the development process in this example. First, money and gold didn't help — in fact, they got in the way. The gold and silver the Israelites carried away from Egypt was used to build two things: the altar and Covenant Box which were aids to worship, and the golden calf, an idol. Wealth is a dangerous resource. In the worst case, money facilitates idolatry, not development.

Second, a whole generation got in the way. This is the sad part of the story. A lifetime of slavery and oppression had been internalized in the hearts and minds of a generation. No matter what miracles God performed, when the stress got high enough the complaint was always the same: "Why did you bring us out of Egypt? We would be better off there." Returning to the way it was — as bad as it was — is sometimes easier to handle than coping with the uncertainty and risk of change. Sometimes, sadly, a whole generation needs to pass away before change is really accepted.

Third, idolatry got in the way. The people got distracted. They forgot who it was that brought them through the significant change. Great care needs to be taken that people do not begin to trust in money or externally supplied skills, nor new knowledge or, worst of all, in an outside organization for their better future.

Lessons for facilitating development

We've looked at the contrast between the people in Egypt and the people after the desert experience. We then looked at some of the things that helped the people get from Egypt to Israel and some of the things that hindered that process. Now we will look at what this might teach us about facilitating development.

First, we must note the importance of an incarnational approach. This was Jesus' model: "The Word became flesh and made his dwelling among us." It was also the model of the liberation of Israel. God went before them day and night in the form of the pillar of cloud and the pillar of fire. God in their midst. A leader of their own kind whom God called and to whom God spoke.

Second, we should underscore the importance of transformed attitude and vision. Oppression, poverty and idolatry all curtail the vision of the people. Such things create eyes that cannot see and ears that cannot hear. The importance of evangelism — appropriate, sensitive and holistic — is critical. This is not a call for the crusading mind of one who arrives from afar to make an announcement and leave. Rather, it is a call for the crucified mind of one who is called to live for a while among others; one who is deeply moved to compassionate action by what he or she sees and hears.

Third, we cannot fail to note the importance of time and patience. It took 40 years to get Egypt out of Israel. Not the five to seven years of a typical development project. Kosuke Koyama, a Japanese theologian, tells us that we have a three-and-a-half mile-an-hour God. By that he means a God who walks only as fast as we can walk. Development does not follow a timetable. It happens when it happens. We in the West commit many sins because we don't fully accept this reality. We have watches and we watch them.

Fourth, money doesn't always help, and it can hinder. Money is almost incidental to the importance of people who come to live and stay the course; to a transformed vision and attitude about what is possible; and to a patient, steadfast view of time.

THE RELATIONSHIP TO HEALTHCARE

Thus far we have focused on human development — what helped Israel, what didn't help, and what we might learn about sustainable development. But what does this mean for healthcare? What lessons might be drawn as we think together about healthcare as a component of development?

Knowing and trusting a God who is with them

> People need a transformed vision of God. They need to know a God who is with them and for them. This means a God who wills health and wholeness. Poor health is *not* his will, nor his punishment.

Following a leader who listens to God

> People need to know that their healthcare practitioner is listening to God. People need to know that his Son and his word are the source of the practitioner's ability to work healing and wholeness. They need to understand that the healthcare they receive is from someone whose faith is in God and not in medical knowledge, skills, and tools.

Learning skills

> This is more obvious. Part of healthcare promotion is the teaching of skills. The challenge is in the *how*. Are skills and knowledge taught in a way in which people are empowered to manage their own healthcare? Or is dependency being taught: dependency on the healthcare profession and its institutions? Are teachers emptying themselves of their knowledge, their power?

Developing kingdom ethics and values

> Health and wholeness are values. Their absence is a result of a lack of justice and a lack of love, not simply a lack of knowledge. There are reasons why people are not well. These reasons often have to do with systems and structures. We must be holistic practitioners — helping the poor understand why they are poor and why they stand outside the healthcare system.

Celebrating culture, beauty and art

> People, poor or rich, need a vision of health and wholeness — of what could and should be — of God's will. This vision must be more than medicine or even psychology provides. This vision must be communicated in ways other than words, especially to the pre-literate poor. Culture and art carry the message of human aspirations and vision. Are we using culture and art? Sustainable health means people whose vision of a better future includes physical and emotional health.

Developing social structure and rules

> Human institutions of health, government, and NGOs are fallen. Created to serve others, they serve themselves. If we wish to change health for the better, healthcare institutions must change too. How do we help healthcare institutions to remember their true vocation?

Hindrances to healthcare

Earlier we mentioned things in the Egypt to Israel story that hindered sustainable development. How might these relate to healthcare?

Money and gold don't help much

> Poor health resulting from lack of money is too simple. The issue is better described in terms of lack of knowledge, access and justice. We know the poor can manage a large proportion of their healthcare with little money.

Another sign of the general non-relevance of money is that if money were the answer, people in the North would be healthy. This is not so. In fact, in the North, money is used not for health but to eat too many of the wrong things and to pollute the water and the air.

A generation got in the way

This is a sad reality, but a reality nonetheless. The question is how to join with the older generation; to care for and help them in a way they can understand, while making the key difference with the younger generation.

Idolatry got in the way

Anything that diverts faith from God to something else is an idol. Care must be taken to avoid having people believe that the key to health and wholeness lies in the healthcare worker. Healthcare workers can become idols; drugs can become a form of magic. Primary healthcare and its workers can be a force for secularization.

Sustainable development through healthcare

Previously, we outlined three fundamental lessons from the Exodus story about facilitating development. They were:

The importance of an incarnational approach

People become whole and are healed in community. Relationships are the key to health. We cannot be instruments of healing from afar. We must go to the people and live among them.

Transformed attitude and vision

Providing things such as medicines, immunizations and education is not enough. People need a new vision. They need liberation from all that hinders them from health and healing; from superstition; from healthcare systems which do not care for them. They need a new vision in which they take responsibility to manage their own healthcare.

Importance of time and patience

We need to take a long view, a people-centered view. Sustainable healthcare by the people will happen when it happens. We need to walk at the pace of the people, not at our pace or the pace of funding.

Unfortunately, Western organizations are often better at raising money than we are in these other three areas. The Exodus story presents such organizations with a challenge — something to think about, to ponder and to pray about.

First, we could decide to become more skilled at finding and developing the kind of people who are willing and qualified to go and live among the poor; to develop those personal relationships that bring about the health and healing of everyone in the relationship.

Second, we could decide to find more and better ways to share the Good News of Jesus Christ, so that the lost among the poor come to know the God who would accompany them on their pilgrimage from Egypt to the Promised Land.

Third, we could seek the help of other cultures to develop an alternative view of time — one that celebrates the fullness of time, the completion of a process. We could decide that, if God is willing to walk at three and a half miles per hour, so could we.

Finally, we could decide to seek God's help in liberating ourselves a little more from a preoccupation with money so that it can take its rightful place as a simple resource, rather than being the measure of what we do.

From Egypt to the Promised Land. Our pilgrimage and the pilgrimage to which rich and poor are invited together. God's journey for us all.

FOUR

COMPASSIONATE CARING AND HEALING

Eric R. Ram

INTRODUCTION

A large portion of Jesus' ministry was devoted to healing. Half of St. Mark's Gospel is devoted to narratives of healing. In the Gospel of St. Luke, Jesus teaches us by the parable of the Good Samaritan that the stranger is our neighbor who deserves not only our love but also our sacrifice.

Health and healing are an integral part of the gospel, are present throughout the Bible and have always been a concern of the church. The Christian understanding of *health* derives from the Christian belief about God's plan for salvation. Health is the harmonious and balanced relationship of the spiritual, physical, mental, social and economic aspects of a person, in harmony with God and with the natural environment. In biblical terms this is known as *shalom*, a state of right relationships.

Salvation is the means by which sinful and fallen men and women are able to return to the wholeness which God desired for them when he created them in his own image. By this process the peace of God extends from God himself to all of his creation, including human beings.

In the ministry of Jesus, healing was a sign of the breaking into human life of the powers of the kingdom of God and of the dethroning of the powers of evil. Healing is the process of reestablishing broken relationships into dynamic, peaceful, harmonious relationships. Body, mind and spirit are inseparable. What happens to one part affects the other.

CALL TO HEALING

One of the most beautiful examples of Christ's compassion for people in need is this depiction in the first chapter of Mark: "Now when it was evening, and the sun had set, they brought unto him all who were ill and who were possessed. And the whole town gathered at the door. And he cured many who were afflicted with various diseases and cast out many devils...." (Mark 1:32-34)

This is a scene repeated many times over. At the end of a day of travel and hard work, hungry, thirsty, dusty from the road, tired and in need of rest, Jesus always had time for people who came to him with their needs. Above all, he had compassion for them and on them.

The Gospels also teach another lesson: concern for the sick and healing for the whole community. The paralyzed, the blind and the deaf were brought to Jesus by their families and friends. It was they who begged Jesus for his help so insistently. At Capernaum they even dug a hole through the roof in someone else's house to lower a paralytic man into Jesus' presence. Christ's acts of healing were, in fact, a community affair. The families and friends of those who were sick shared in the experience of healing.

By common usage, the word "health" is associated with medical care. One of the more persistent beliefs about health has been that the availability of more medical care — more doctors and more hospitals — would result in better health. That concept is now changing.

Throughout the world the problems of ill health are strongly related to, and dependent on, factors such as poverty, poor housing, poor environment, lack of safe drinking water, lack of food, malnutrition, under-nutrition, high fertility rates, illiteracy, unemployment and low income, land tenure and inaccessibility of social services.

Despite the "magic" of modern medicine and daily pronouncements of major breakthroughs in medical technology, the most basic health needs of the majority of the world's people are not met in even a rudimentary manner. On the other hand, our dependency on modern technology has increased so much that we are forgetting the human aspects of healing.

Reconciliation, hope and compassion have a key role to play in the healing process. How do we integrate these important healing ingredients into our medical and health care?

We get so busy with our daily work, writing project proposals, getting funds and managing them, making reports, etc., that the impor-tant task of making healthcare available to the ones who need it most seems to slacken, and we have a tendency to slide into a life style that is money-driven or achievement-driven. We need to be compelled by compassion, as our Lord was. "Be compassionate as your Father is compassionate" (Luke 6:36), and put our priorities into proper perspective.

The meaning of compassion

Compassion has been the recurring theme of Christ's own acts of healing. We need to understand that compassion is more than pity or sympathy. It transcends social work, health work, philanthropy and all governmental and non-governmental programs. It is the capacity to feel and suffer with persons in need, to experience something of their predicaments, fears, anxieties and temptations; the loss of freedom and dignity, the utter vulnerability, the assault on the whole person and the alienation poverty and illness produce and portend.

Compassion is more than a feeling. It flows over in a willingness to help, to sacrifice, to go out of one's way as the Good Samaritan did. None of us can help anyone without entering fully into the painful situation the other person is in, without taking the risk of becoming hurt or getting wounded in the process.

Compassion entails understanding in-depth the suffering experienced by another. When we have suffered ourselves, we are usually better able to understand it in others. An Indian proverb says, "Illness tells you who you are," or, as Miguel de Unamuno (a Spanish author) says, "Suffering is the substance of life and the root of personality, for only suffering makes us persons."

In addition, compassion helps us realize that our brothers and sisters in need are not alien to us. They are very much fellow travelers on this planet Earth. I have found that they, in fact, are vital to our own spiritual renewal and growth. Healthcare "providers" need the needy to humanize them as much as healthcare needs to be humanized. Compassionate care is never a unilateral act or a one way street. Our lives are bound to be affected because the lives of others are intricately interwoven with ours.

Love and hope

Paul, in his letter to the Galatians, lists a number of what he calls the fruit of the Spirit (Galatians 5:22-23). Dr. Paul Brand, a globally known medical missionary and surgeon, calls these a polyvalent vaccine for the prevention of almost all diseases that have behavioral bases. This polyvalent vaccine includes Love, Joy, Peace, Patience, Gentleness, Goodness, Faithfulness, Humility and Self-Control. If people were only willing to be filled with the Spirit and bring forth the fruit of the Spirit, how much healthier we all would be.

From his own experience Dr. Bernie Siegel, an oncologist and surgeon from Yale University, says that love, joy and peace of mind have physiological consequences, just as depression and despair do. The contribution of a life style and the emotions to the health of the individual was a concept easily accepted centuries ago.

Today, people want "scientific" proof. Feelings have to be shown to create chemical alterations in our bodies in order for us to accept them as physiological. Fortunately, we have the scientific know-how to document those changes.

We have learned over the years that body, mind and spirit are one unit and that what happens to one affects the other. Body and mind seem bound by nerves and messenger molecules allowing them to communicate.

Psychologists have shown that the effects of love on the body can be measured: an unloved infant will have retarded bone growth and may even die early. A stroked infant, on the other hand, grows faster. People who meditate regularly and confide their traumatic experiences to diaries rather than repressing them are shown to have an enhanced immune function.

Love and peace of mind do protect us and allow us to overcome the problems life brings our way. Anything that offers hope has the potential to heal, including thoughts, suggestions, symbols, and placebos. Some experiments have shown that the administration of placebos leads to an increased production in the brain of endorphins, which are pain killers.

Scientists are searching for other chemicals which are produced in our brain as a response to various feelings and may become the basis of many therapies in the future. Norman Cousins says that the will to live is most important, enabling the body to make the most of placebos. Placebos then play the role of emissary between the will to live and the body.

Nero Asistent is one of the few known long-term AIDS survivors. She has managed to reverse the results of a test from HIV positive to HIV negative. Asked to summarize her successful efforts she says: "When you live in your heart, magic happens." Though the precise mechanisms of the healing response remain elusive, many factors work to create body-mind-spirit communication and unity, thus bringing body functions under the control of mind and spirit.

We have known for some time that both environment and genes play a significant role in a person's vulnerability to certain diseases, but the emotional environment we create within our bodies through compassion, love, hope and peace activate mechanisms of healing. Every person has the potential and ability to create such an environment within his or her body to facilitate healing.

God has placed within us a never-ending desire to love and be loved. He has also given us a never-ending supply of people to love. We need to love ourselves and we need to love others because, in the process, we experience healing just as much as do those who are sick.

Implications for health professionals

We Christians must recognize with the utmost humility that compassion is a human quality present in non-Christians as well. What is different for Christians is that compassion is an obedient response to a loving Father and not a notable act of self-sacrifice.

For the health professional, compassion is the quality that separates a mere career from Christian vocation. The compassionate health professional recognizes that illness transcends biological aberrations in our body's systems and fractures our image of ourselves, upsets harmony and balance and begins to destroy us. We also see man's illness as a sign that he has fallen away from God's order.

Compassion, hope, love and peace enable the healing process to mend and reconstruct a person, to make him or her "whole" again. We must assist in the healing of the hurt spirit as well as the attack on the body. Compassionate care also means that we help a person die in dignity if he or she is suffering from a terminal disease. Further, compassionate care is not limited only to an individual person but extends to the entire community.

BUILDING A HEALING COMMUNITY

Dr. Robert A. Lambourne, a British physician and theologian who promoted the concept of wholeness in the early sixties, saw in the act of healing a close parallel to the sacrament of the eucharist by which the church sustains herself and her members through the body and blood of her Lord and is continually renewed.

In every act of healing Christ regarded himself as a representative of the community, which participated with him then and still should through his body, the church. It is the Christian congregation as a whole which is meant to be the healing body of Christ among men and women, and *can* be when we have effectively become a community knit together in him.

For some time now, churches have left the ministry of healing in the hands of a few professionals who are more involved in curing disease than in healing the whole person, which goes beyond the treatment of physical and mental illness, and certainly beyond doctors and nurses.

The entire congregation, the entire community, can become a support system in the process of healing. In fact, the congregation can become a healing community. Illness is itself disruptive of the community. God is the healer not just of individuals, but of the entire community. The whole community in turn must participate in its own healing.

The resources we have in the form of medical and health knowledge are not proprietary. They are held in trust by professionals. They must be freely shared with others. Sharing of knowledge also means sharing of power. There is a saying in the Hindi language which says, "The only thing you save in this life is what you give away."

There is a need to demystify medicine and technology. Medical and health knowledge need to be put in simple and understandable language backed up by appropriate technology. Making people aware of their rights and responsibilities helps them determine their own health priorities and take part in solving their own health problems. This is an essential step in the process of the empowerment of people for their own health.

Providing medical and health facilities has a minimal effect unless there is an adequate supply of nutritious food, safe water, shelter and a clean environment. These basic needs are interdependent and cannot be seen in isolation. It is the lack of a healthy environment rather than the lack of medical intervention that subjects the greater part of the world's population to the constant threat of infection.

No matter how imaginative or economically viable a healthcare project may be in the eyes of its designer, it will not take root if it is designed for the people rather than with the people. A word of advice to the planners: Mahatma Gandhi said, "Recall the face of the poorest and the most helpless man whom you may have seen and ask yourself if the step you contemplate is going to be of any use to him." People have to participate in the decisions which affect their lives.

About 4,000 meters up in the Andes, I saw a project in which a Quichua Indian community worked together with World Vision Ecuador and the government to obtain safe drinking water. The community dug trenches, laid pipes, and provided land and labor; World Vision provided the technical know-how and the materials (the pipes), while the government paid for the water tank.

They worked for six months on this project and in the end got clear, safe, sparkling water from a large spring ten kilometers away. As a result, they have practically wiped out diarrhea and other water-borne diseases from that community.

Through compassionate care, we also have to rehabilitate and revitalize traditional values, traditional foods and herbal medicines that people have lost in the process of modernization or "westernization." For instance, I have seen indigenous people sell milk to buy Coca-Cola, sell eggs to buy chiclitos (chewing gum) and sell quinoa (a high-protein grain found in the Andes) to buy spaghetti. We must restore human dignity to people, along with the traditional values that are solid and good and have sustained them for centuries.

Sometimes we set up systems and structures for our convenience, but these cannot take the place of the caring aspect of our health services. We have to collect certain data to monitor progress but remember, people do not want to be and cannot be treated as objects. They have to be full and equal partners in the healing process. An old Indian man in a remote village once told me: "My blood is also red like yours." How true! We are created equal and in the image of God.

Compassion, hope, peace and love are important ingredients with effects that go beyond physical healing. Compassionate care is a process by which we participate in the suffering and pain of another person and in return we are spiritually renewed and enriched as well. No medicine can do that.

DATE DUE

MR 9 '92			
AP 7 '92			
DE 21 '92			
NO 4 '94			
DE 6 '94			
DE 17 '97			

```
BT                    35600
732
.A44       Allen, E. Anthony
1991          Health, healing, and
           transformation.
```

HIEBERT LIBRARY
Fresno Pacific College - M.B. Seminary
Fresno, CA 93702